WATCHING MYSELF
BE BORDERLINE

A Smart Sufferer Says
How It Started And How She Survives

D1603100

JANSEN VEE

outskirts
press

Outskirts Press, Inc.
http://www.outskirtspress.com

ISBN: 978-1-9772-3187-1

Cover Image by White Horse Graphics & Printing

Outskirts Press and the "OP" logo are trademarks belonging to Outskirts Press, Inc.

PRINTED IN THE UNITED STATES OF AMERICA

Table of Contents

Dedication

I DEDICATE THIS book to those who have suffered the confusing pain of growing up in families that appeared, both to the outside observer and to the inside participants, to be sort of normal, but were not.

Foreword

JANSEN VEE'S ACCOUNT of her life should be read as a critical exploration of a person's journey of choosing life or death.

Depression and mental illness are often blamed as causes of suicide; as a result, suicide prevention policymaking is firmly placed within mental health services. Suicide prevention policies are based on the assumption that depression and/or mental illness is present in suicidal cases. With this approach, suicide is never addressed, because the focus of suicide intervention is to seek out, diagnose, and treat a mental illness or depression. This method is not preventative for the main reason that it relies on intervention only after a mental illness has manifested itself or when suicide has been attempted.

Suicide is not a new social and health concern. Suicide research involving analyses of historical, religious documents, and literature[1] provides accounts of suicide due to various causes but rarely because of mental illness. Suicide is mystifying because, firstly, for the living, it is hard to comprehend ending one's own life, and secondly, why, despite advancements in medicine, has suicide not been eradicated?

Over the last century or so, suicide has been medicalized and firmly placed within the domain of psychiatry as a mental illness. As a result, most suicide research is biased because there is the assumption of the presence of mental illness and/or depression from the outset. Unfortunately, the problem is that researchers have consistently failed to account or correct for such biases.

Repeated data on suicide outcomes are necessary to gain insight into suicide. The problem with suicide research is that death only occurs once. On average between two-thirds and three-quarters of all suicide cases are successful in their first attempt – therefore, we know nothing about this group's social and health status and their process of decision-making.

For the other one-quarter to one-third who failed to complete suicide initially, intervention methods focus on diagnosing and treating a mental illness. Yet, this group still went on to complete suicide. So the question as to why some people choose death over life whilst other people with similar characteristics choose life over death is never addressed and explained. Only when we have insight into an individual's process of decision-making can we develop effective suicide prevention strategies.

Our current knowledge of suicide and mental illness raises more questions than answers, making prevention and intervention policies irrelevant and inappropriate. In a recent book–Shahtahmasebi and Omar (2020), *The Broader View of Suicide*, Cambridge Scholars Publishing–we argue that research shows that mental illness is not the cause of suicide, and that suicide prevention policies based on assuming the presence of mental illness are not working. Suicide data suggest that it is not wise to assume that there is one single adverse life event that causes suicide. Suicide occurs in groups where mental illness is present but also in groups where mental illness is not present; individuals who are bereaved attempt suicide but so do those who are not bereaved; unemployed individuals commit suicide but so do those still employed; and so on.

It is not surprising that decades of using a mental illness approach to suicide prevention has failed to prevent suicide and failed to reduce national and global suicide rates. In 2018, the United States Center for Disease Control and Prevention[2] (CDC) warned of the rising suicide rate in the USA and across the globe[3].

Research also shows that non-medical approaches performed at a grassroots level have a much better chance of successfully preventing suicide.

This book should be read in the above context. Jansen Vee's life story enables an exploration of suicide as an outcome of a decision-making process, while at the same time examines life with mental illness.

In March 2020, in response to one of my papers on suicide in which I argued that we do not know the process of decision-making of most suicide cases because they were successful in completing suicide in their first attempt, Jansen contacted me and offered her life story to shed some light to help understand the process of decision-making which leads to suicide. She has been providing updates ever since. I was surprised but delighted when she invited me to write a Foreword for her first book. In writing this piece I am mainly focusing on suicide rather than mental illness.

Jansen bravely writes about her life to describe her decision-making process. She is candid about herself and her life. Her analysis of her own life events and herself as a human being who frequently considers committing suicide leads the reader to understand her process of decision-making as it relates to her life ordeal, which has been explained as mental illness.

Jansen accepts and seems to take comfort in, the fact that the medical approach had mapped her life into a series of mental illness diagnoses. Jansen admits that receiving conventional treatments: psychiatric, cognitive therapy, and counseling, for most of that period, had done nothing to alleviate her symptoms. She still felt suicidal following medication and treatment. Jansen's suicidality manifested late in her life – in all probability as a result of the medical interventions for her mental illnesses: she recalls feeling suicidal after taking prescribed medications.

Jansen's experiences provide an example of how medicalizing behavior when one illness category does not fit the symptoms then creates more. Jansen expresses the wish for an alternative, non-medical approach culture, where the community as a whole is part of the solution to improve and support mental well-being for people who need it.

A grassroots approach to protect and support vulnerable people in the community is very rare in the medicalized Western world which tends to leave individuals to either face their dilemmas alone or accept medical intervention. Jansen's account provides insight into the reasons why some individuals may refuse medical help.

Society and communities are often let off the hook by describing suicide as a sudden death which occurs without warning. Policy-makers and service-providers across the globe frequently claim that if they had advanced knowledge of mental illness, they could have intervened and prevented suicide. In this book, Jansen's life story challenges such claims. A suicide attempt is not sudden to the majority of adult suicide cases. Individuals often provide signs about their suicidality, such as changes in behavior, or out-of-character behavior, but very few people talk about death directly. We tend to miss the signs for suicide and dismiss talk of death as spiritual beliefs or as personal opinion. Suicide has been kept under wraps in the psychiatric/psychology domain for so long that the public, various professionals, and medical staff have no idea about suicide discourse and behavior.

Interestingly, in telling her life story, Jansen expresses a desire for some form of community involvement in supporting people with mental illness and suicidality. Her process of decision-making was not influenced by her mental illness, but by the mental health services she sought help from. Not only has her mental illness not been alleviated or treated, but also Jansen has been given additional mental illness diagnoses.

Jansen's life story clearly indicates that she does not want to die by suicide, but that she feels suicide may be inevitable. Perhaps an explanation for this feeling lies in Jansen's many examples of mental health interventions/treatments she has received. Jansen seeks psychiatric help at the first sign of suicidality, but the medical interventions she receives often fail to pay sufficient attention to her suicidality.

I highly recommend this book to everyone, from psychiatric/psychology practitioners to medical professionals to the general public. This book makes an important contribution to our discourse on suicide.

Said Shahtahmasebi, PhD
July 2010
The Good Life Research Centre Trust
https://journalofhealth.co.nz/

[1]   (e.g. see suicide in 1001 nights https://journalofhealth.co.nz/?page_id=2153, also see archives of Dynamics of Human Health www.journalofhealth.co.nz).

[2]   https://www.cdc.gov/vitalsigns/suicide/

[3]   https://journalofhealth.co.nz/?page_id=1681

Acknowledgments

I AM GRATEFUL for the weekly conversations that I have had with my writing coach and editor, Douglas Winslow Cooper, which have enabled me to remain cheerful and motivated as I have written this book. I am grateful for the insight and analysis of Said Shahtahmasebi and for his contribution of the Foreword to this book. I thank my housekeeper, Jennifer Kohler, for doing uninteresting tasks so that I could do more interesting tasks. Also, I appreciate the support I have received over the years from the Cedar Hills United Church of Christ and the recent support from St. Andrew Lutheran Church.

Preface

FOR SEVERAL DECADES, I had unsatisfactory conversations with people about my family of origin.

I would attempt to tell them about the terrible pain I was experiencing as I thought about growing up with my parents. But I would get dismissive or unhelpful responses such as, "All parents make mistakes" or "I'm sure your mother did the best she could."

After a long while, I came to realize that the stories I had to tell about my family of origin did not carry much of an impact. I had no story of being beaten; no one had sexually abused me. The stories I had to tell sounded like I was saying that some small thing had gone wrong in my family life. It was almost impossible to impress upon people how devastating the behavior of my parents toward me was.

Then I learned about invalidation. I learned that certain kinds of children are profoundly harmed when their parents are not able to see them for who they really are and affirm them in their uniqueness. Actually, invalidation is bad for all children. But certain children do extremely poorly when they are raised by invalidating parents.

I have a story about my mother that requires 20 minutes to be told. At the end of the story, I relate that my mother looked into my 10-year-old face and said, "I'm so glad that we have enough money to buy fresh vegetables." Without the 20 minutes of lead-up to this quotation, one would never guess that this is a profound invalidation of little Jansen — but it is. And even the 20-minute story does not impress a person who is determined not to hear anything bad about my mother when listening to the story.

My motivation in writing this book is to tell my story about a family that seemed to be kind of normal, when observed either from the outside (that is, the family as seen, for example, attending church together) or observed from the inside (that is, the family as seen, for example, eating dinner together with no one else present).

I have told my story of a family that was deeply invalidating, a family that damaged me terribly, even though the damage requires quite a bit of explanation. If you are interested in the way that borderline personality disorder develops, you will find this enlightening. If you have wondered about some family that impressed you as strangely not-quite-right, but in some way that was hard to express, you may find this enlightening. If you have seen a family that takes care of children yet does not take care of children, you may recognize certain behaviors in this writing.

I have tried to present a balanced view of the damaged people involved and the damage that happened. No one is at fault in the story — it is a sad unfolding of unfortunate circumstances. But there is the possibility of identifying the damage that was done and facing it straightforwardly. This I continue to do.

Jansen Vee
Autumn 2020

Disclaimer

IT IS NECESSARY to be careful using this book.

In this book, I address the characteristics of a mental illness called "borderline personality disorder." In one section of the book, I use a list that comes from a document, *DSM-IV*, which until recently was used by professionals when diagnosing borderline personality disorder in a person who is suffering.

The process of diagnosing mental illness in a human being is complicated and involves much more than looking at some characteristics on a list. Professional people go through a period of education and subsequent training that is like an apprenticeship, during which they study with someone who is experienced at diagnosing and treating people with mental illness.

This brings me to my comment on the care that must be taken with this book: recognizing characteristics in oneself or another person from reading this book is of no significance, clinically. That is, reading a book will not allow you to figure out who has or does not have borderline personality disorder.

Please, do not misuse my book! Be careful. A lot of harm can come from deciding that someone has a mental illness or does not have a mental illness without consulting a reputable professional in whom you can trust.

CHAPTER 1
My Favorite Suzy Story

WHEN MY MOTHER, Suzy, died, we held her memorial service at my church, and we had to print extra bulletins. We had to print extra bulletins because so many people showed up. Suzy was so successful at only-on-the-surface relationships with neighbors, coworkers, and others that more people showed up than we anticipated.

That story is my older sister's favorite Suzy story. She loves it because it demonstrates how completely Suzy was able to fool people and how unlikely it was that anyone would have believed her three daughters if they had tried to speak their truth. (The pastor helped us fashion a memorial service in which we did not speak a single word of our truth — although the pastor slid in some references to our truth here and there, bless her heart.)

My favorite Suzy story is the Christmas Gift Story. This is a story I heard my mother, Suzy, tell at least five times in my adult life. She would tell it at parties and family gatherings as if it were amusing. A Thanksgiving gathering that included some of my 17 cousins on her side of the family would have been a perfect setting for this story.

"I was walking across the quad on the university campus," Suzy would say, "just before Christmas when I was in graduate school." The fact that she always told the story with a reference to graduate school allows me to know that I would have been 13 years old.

Suzy would continue, "I was telling one of my friends about my preparations for Christmas — how I had purchased for each of my three girls a book, a piece of clothing, a toy, and a board game." Then Suzy would explain that her friend had replied by asking, "But, what do the girls *want* for Christmas?"

Looking around at her audience, Suzy would say with a smile, "I had never thought about what the girls *wanted* for Christmas! I didn't know I was supposed to. I had never realized I was supposed to ask them what they wanted for Christmas!" Then she would laugh in a manner that invited others to laugh along with her as she, once again, glanced around the room.

Many people would laugh along politely, but there were always some faces that betrayed puzzlement. What was the source of Suzy's delight?

Suzy was relating an *Aha!* experience; that is, she was telling of a time she had suddenly understood a previously not-understood problem or concept. Suzy parented according to hundreds of rules (well, I don't really know how many rules) that she had learned from books and from observing others and from talking to others. She was describing her delight at having learned another rule. Not unlike a child discovering that subtraction undoes addition, she was trying to share her pleasure at having put a piece in place in her intellectual scheme for good parenting.

The puzzled looks on some of the faces resulted from what was for others the *non sequitur* of the jump from Suzy's friend's asking what the girls wanted for Christmas to Suzy's delight. Since most people do not parent according to rules, or at least not explicit rules that they could write down for you, they do not experience intellectual pleasure when their parenting scheme acquires a new and beautiful piece of the puzzle.

Suzy had a deep commitment to parenting in a manner different from the way she was parented. For that, she deserves a great deal of credit — more credit really than words can express. But she, herself, had been so badly damaged by the parenting she had received that she was not able to be guided very much by any inner sense of kindness and compassion.

Being a very intelligent person and a very good thinker, Suzy acquired for herself rules for everything. This is the reason that each child received for Christmas a book, a piece of clothing, a toy, and a board game. This is what each child received every year. We received these four gifts year after year after year after year. We never received a piece of candy. No candy canes. No socks or mittens. No handmade Christmas cards nor notes of affection. No handmade coupons for a favorite dinner. Apparently, no one she spoke to had ever said anything that caused her to create a rule that candy was supposed to be purchased for Christmas. (Suzy did not eat candy.)

So, the point of her story, my favorite Suzy story, was that she had acquired a new rule: *a good mommy asks her children what they want for Christmas.*

The energy behind her story that caused her to laugh with delight was the energy of the intellectual pleasure of having built her parenting rule system into a better rule system.

The reason I love this story is that it gives such insight into Suzy.

Presumably, I had received about 13 birthday gifts by this time and about 13 sets of Christmas gifts. Never had she, in selecting any of those gifts, considered what I might want. It had simply never occurred to her to think about what I might want.

This tells us a lot about Suzy. And, from a lot of other information that I have analyzed over the 45 years that I have been in psychotherapy, I have learned that she was excessively narcissistic. The damage that had occurred in her first few years of life and then throughout her childhood was so severe that she knew that she wanted and needed things, but she did not know that any other creature wanted and needed things. She wanted and needed things and everything else in the world was a tool either doing or not doing what she wanted it to do at any given moment. Some of those tools walked and talked.

One does not ask a tool what she wants for Christmas. One does not ask a tool what she wants for her birthday. To be a good mommy to a tool is to follow the rules for good mommy-hood. To find out the rules for good parenthood, Suzy read books and asked other mothers and tried not to do what was done to her.

Let me say again that Suzy deserves credit for trying not to do what was done to her. If I were to write that a thousand times, it would not be enough. Suzy had one overwhelming goal in her life: to appear to the world to be a good mother. In order to maintain the appearance of being a good mother, she strove to be, actually, a good mother. She was wildly incapable of being a good mother. However, I cannot overstate it: she really meant to be.

Let me also say that does not excuse the damage that she did to me; nor have I any plans to forgive her. And I will tell you why.

CHAPTER 2

Forgiveness and Non-Forgiveness

IT SOUNDS HARSH, doesn't it? I have no intention of forgiving my parents.

Forgiveness can happen in many different ways. I have been part of the Christian tradition for my entire 60-year life. The Christian tradition has a rich history of theology and has a wonderful plethora of living theologians. This provides many ideas about forgiveness consistent with Christian thought. And, if one expands one's thinking to the world's enduring religions, there are even more ideas about human forgiveness to choose from.

Forgiveness between two people who have a strong and positive relationship can be an easy thing. However, my relationship with my mother consisted of trauma bonds surrounded later by bonds created by attempts to build an adult relationship. Similarly, my relationship with my father began with bonds that were not loving bonds and was later complicated by attempts to create something good from something broken.

Neither of my parents perceived that there was anything for which they needed to be forgiven. There was no repentance or sorrow on their part. They might have been defensive if they had been willing, at all, to talk about what had happened in my childhood.

As you might imagine, the interactions I had with my parents as an adult also further damaged our relationships. Let me give you some examples:

I did not receive gifts from my father for my birthday or Christmas after my mother made him leave our home, until he met his second wife, Sunny. Then she told him that he was required to give his daughters birthday and Christmas gifts. For Christmas in 1980, my father gave me a wool sweater, a cardigan, decorated with a lovely Norwegian pattern.

The sweater was not quite big enough. After opening the gift, I tried it on and said, "Oh, it's not quite big enough. But I'm sure they have one in a bigger size."

"Well, no," Bill said, producing his little laugh that indicated he was uncomfortable, "it was on the sale rack, so it can't be returned."

There was a pause — some silence in the room. I allowed the silence for a moment to see if he was going to offer to buy me something that did fit. I waited, hoping he might apologize for buying something that I could not use. He did not say any more words. Apparently, the fact that he had bought me something that I could not use, and he could not return, was not any kind of problem for him.

"Well," I said, "I can probably use my sewing machine to make it into something really pretty."

Notice here that I am taking care of my father's emotional needs. My father has made a mistake, and he is uncomfortable. He is not able to respond to the situation in an adult-like manner to take action that would be appropriate to correct his error. It is up to the daughter, admittedly now an adult, to soothe the father's distress, to be satisfied with the inadequate gift, to make sure the family Christmas goes on uninterrupted.

This did not improve my relationship with my father, and there was no possibility of talking to him later, hoping he would understand what had happened and ask me for forgiveness.

Here's another example of an interaction, this time with my mother, that damaged our relationship:

Suzy had moved, after retiring, to a house three miles away from mine so that she could enjoy time with her grandson, my only child. It was Christmas and my boy, Pat, was about five years old. Suzy was invited to come over very early Christmas morning to be included in the opening of gifts. We tolerated her inability to allow two people to open gifts at the same time. In the most loving manner we could, we participated in her nonstop question-and-answer chatter as the gifts were opened.

After the gifts had all been opened, my husband, Mark, and Pat and I went into the kitchen to work on breakfast. A little bit later, I stepped into the living room expecting to see the Christmas tree and the new toys and the wonderful riot of bows and ribbons and Christmas wrapping, but — behold! The room was in an amazingly sterile state of orderliness.

Suzy had taken all of the fun and chaos of Christmas and obliterated it. She had lined up the toys and folded every bit of wrapping and put all the bows into a tiny little bag. You couldn't tell that Christmas had even happened.

"You cleaned everything up," I said in an unhappy voice.

Perceiving that I was not pleased, she was terribly apologetic, but bizarrely. This did not improve my relationship with Suzy, and there was no possibility of talking to her, hoping she would understand and ask for forgiveness. She was only able to feel unwelcome and unappreciated and accused of having wanted to destroy my Christmas. She was not able to be sorry for inadvertently taking away something I wanted. She could be a martyr. She could be the victim. But she could not grasp that she had made a mistake.

Clearly, the kind of forgiveness that requires a strong, positive relationship between two people was never going to happen with me and either Bill or Suzy.

But there is another kind of Christian forgiveness that comes from one side and flows to the other side. This is the kind of forgiveness some people can give when someone has harmed them, but the person does not understand or feel any regret or remorse. This freely given forgiveness can be an unburdening for the forgiver. But it must be true forgiveness. Pretend forgiveness doesn't count.

Sometimes people who only poorly understand Christianity encourage people who have been harmed to *pretend forgive* the person who harmed them. When I say *pretend forgive*, I mean for them to speak words that sound as if they have forgiven the perpetrator and to live as though they do not feel anger or resentment toward the person who damaged them. This is not forgiveness; this is play-acting forgiveness.

It is a terrible burden to put upon someone who is already the recipient of bad treatment — adding this expectation that they act as if they have undergone an inner transformation of forgiving the perpetrator.

The moment that I actually feel transformed inside — the moment I feel forgiveness well up inside of me — I will live from that new orientation of having forgiven my parents. But until it is a reality, I am not going to pretend that it is a reality. Neither Bill nor Suzy ever asked for my forgiveness. Neither of them believed they had anything to regret. Neither of them ever expressed any remorse for anything they had done that harmed me. They both felt that it was unfortunate that the situation developed the way it did, but neither of them thought they had, themselves, done anything wrong.

Of course, in a sense, they did not mean to do anything wrong. Bill was incapable of offering to buy me a second Christmas present. Money was more important to him than his daughter was. As sad as it is to say that, it was true. So he was, in a sense, doing the best he could. Suzy could not tolerate disorder. She was incapable of choosing to leave. She was incapable of staying if the room was not brought into submission. Her comfort was more important to her than her daughter's enjoyment of Christmas. As sad as it is to say that, it was true. So she was, in a sense, doing the best she could.

I don't care. The fact that my parents were doing the best they could does not excuse them from having terribly harmed me. People who deliberately burn their children with cigarettes are also doing the best they can. And we take their children away from them.

These two examples, which happened when I was an adult, are very much like things that happened when I was a child, of course. My first memory goes back to when Suzy and Bill were living in Canada with their three little girls. They were in Canada because Bill was starting a church, a mission church, which means a brand-new church, in a suburb of a Canadian province.

I was born in Canada, although Suzy and Bill were both US citizens, so I have citizenship in both countries (how lucky for me). We moved back to the United States when I was five years old, so I know that this memory comes from my young years, before age five.

I recall Suzy standing in the kitchen and Bill standing in the dining room with the dining room table between them. They were yelling at each other, which didn't impress me because it was the usual situation. Suzy threw a knife at Bill, and Bill ducked to avoid being hit by the knife. This is my first memory of life.

Other memories of life in Canada include a recollection of going downstairs where Bill was sitting at his workbench sorting out his nails. Suzy had, in a fit of anger, gone to his workbench and dumped out all of the different-sized nails into one big pile. I recall going downstairs and offering to help Bill sort the nails. What a pathetic memory! I was probably four years old, and already I was trying to solve the problems of these two troubled adults.

A third memory from Canada has me standing in the bathroom as Suzy is combing my hair, and I am asking Suzy, "When are we going to move?" This is an interesting memory because, along with remembering where I was and what I said, I remember that I knew at the time that I was ingratiating myself to Suzy with the question because Suzy wanted to move to the United States and Bill did not. I was, presumably, four years old, and I was already trying to assure Suzy that I was on her side.

I am not prepared to forgive those big people who didn't notice anxious little Jansen trying to mediate their fighting. They showed no signs of understanding that any harm had come to me.

CHAPTER 3
Fifty Years Before My Time

Or: Do I Really Have a Mental Illness?

MY MOTHER AND father damaged me severely. No, there is no visible damage. If you saw me in the grocery store, you would not see scars on my face from cigarette burns inflicted by my parents or see me walking with a limp from damage to my spine as a result of having been shaken or beaten as an infant. However, my parents damaged me severely.

Suzy and Bill were, coincidentally, each the oldest of five in their families. Suzy, as I have said, had as her highest life goal to maintain the appearance of being a good mother. Bill's highest life goal was, well, I don't know.

Probably it was to feel secure by making a lot of money.

Neither Bill nor Suzy, both of whom have died now, had any idea that they had damaged their children. Neither of them was ever willing to enter into any conversation about the negative effects of their parenting or even discuss any specific event from my childhood. Suzy and Bill and my two sisters and I were like five people who had survived a plane crash together — we were bonded together by the trauma of the experience of our horrible family. There were no bonds of love (or at least I am not aware of any). There were only the bonds of people who

11

somehow had managed to survive a situation that was stressful and frightening day after day after day.

Although I have been diagnosed with quite a number of mental illnesses over the years, the one that resulted from the constant stress and fear of my infancy and childhood is "borderline personality disorder." There is a crucial time of life in the development of the human brain that is related to human bonding and human connection. It comes after birth and stretches to sometime before a baby's first birthday.

Many people who have studied child development know about the child-language-acquisition phase. There is a certain time in the life of a human child when she or he is able to learn a language in a way that is different than the way I, at age 60 now, could learn a new language. In this child-language-acquisition phase, the brain is especially ready to absorb human language. In the evolution of this creature which is the human being, the ability to learn a language quickly and easily at some stage of development must have been a survival advantage. All around the world, little human beings go through a stage in which they just learn a language quickly.

In a similar manner, in the first year of life, babies develop the part of the brain that causes us to say about human beings, "People are wired for human connection." But this wiring does not always successfully develop. And this is one of the ways in which my parents harmed me: my family of origin was so filled with stress and fearfulness that the part of my brain for human connection did not develop.

Of course, there are many, many babies born into families that are filled with stress and fearfulness. Just a moment's thought will lead to the obvious conclusion that not all of them become mentally ill. My mental illness has been extremely debilitating; not all of those many, many babies born into families that are stressful and scary become adults who do not function well enough to be considered mentally healthy.

What was different about me?

Before I tell you what was different about me, there is a larger question to consider — and it is a very big question: am I really mentally ill?

Certainly, it is undeniable that I do not connect with other human beings in the same way that the majority of the population does. Certainly, it is undeniable that I do not function well in some significant areas of physical, emotional, and social self-care which we expect from an adult person. However, if one were to look at human societies throughout the world and over time, the concept of mental illness is not a concept that is pervasive and recurring.

The behavior I exhibit which can be different than most of the population and the experiences I report which can be different than most of the population can be understood in many ways. A woman I know who grew up in Africa (she braids my hair and braids in extensions for me) tells me that her African village culture would not identify me as being ill or defective. I would be cared for in her village in Africa in a different manner than some other person, but simply seen as someone who requires a different type of care.

Although I have not researched this carefully, I have heard a few stories that suggest that some types of behaviors and experiences which we describe today in the United States as mental illness symptoms have been seen by other cultures as indications of special insights or abilities.

The two preceding examples give a positive spin to behaviors and experiences that are now identified as a mental illness in my culture. But there are, of course, many examples of people with nonstandard behaviors and experiences being subjected to horrific treatment because they are different. Dorothea Dix traveled from town to town in New England in the 1800s gathering information about how mentally ill people were being housed and cared for. Although there was an occasional example of wonderfully compassionate care, what she saw was almost uniformly discouraging. She was responsible for establishing state hospitals. At the time, that was a fabulous improvement.

So, do I really have a mental illness? Here's how I think about it:

There was a time in the United States when, to speak broadly about the culture in general, we thought we knew something about a person if their skin was black. That is, if many of the person's forebears had come from Africa as slaves, we thought we knew a lot about the person. And there was a time that we thought we knew a lot about a person if she was married and had small children. We thought we knew she would want to be a homemaker and not feel any desire to pursue a career. There was a time (again speaking in generalities about the culture in the United States) when we thought people who felt a romantic attraction to someone of the same sex were defective or broken.

There was a time when we thought that anyone who experienced themselves in a manner that contrasted with the gender they were assigned at birth was mistaken or wrong.

My observation is that there has been a movement of discovery in the United States. We seem to be discovering that there are more kinds of people than we imagined. The astounding diversity of humanity seems to have taught us that we learn nothing about a person from the color of their skin or the shape of their skull. Intelligence and physical strength correspond little or not at all to appearance in human beings. Desire to nurture children does not suppress the human need for other kinds of fulfilling work in female adults. Adult human beings have a much greater variety of romantic attractions than we had thought.

People experience themselves in relation to our gender constructions in more ways than we had imagined.

(I speak only of the dominant culture in the United States as I have experienced it in the suburban Pacific Northwest. I do not travel outside of the United States, and my mental illness prevents me from exposing myself to many of the available sources of information that would allow me to speak to these issues in a broader context. My PTSD is easily triggered.)

Having said all of this, I am almost ready to answer the question, "Do I have a mental illness?"

First, imagine with me the following scenario. Imagine it is 1970. Imagine you are living, as I was, in a suburb of a city in the Pacific Northwest. A 14-year-old person makes an appointment and goes to see the pastor of their rather large Lutheran Church and explains that although "she" was identified at birth as a girl, they do not experience themselves as a girl. Indeed, they experience themselves as, well, not a girl.

"It's not that I feel like a boy," they say, "I just don't feel like a girl at all."

Imagine the pastor answers, "Yes, I've heard about this. This is a human experience that people have. What we will need to do is educate the entire congregation about people who are questioning their gender identity. We will train the whole congregation to refer to you with *they* and *them*. We will be sure to incorporate some hymns into our worship that have appropriate language so that you will feel welcome."

Would this have happened in 1970? No, in 1970 it was 50 years too soon. In 1970 the pastor would not, probably, already have known about this human experience. There would not have been any way to educate an entire congregation about questioning gender identity. No one would have already written hymns with non-sexist and non-gender-specific language.

In a similar manner, imagine it is 2017. Imagine I am living, as I was, in a suburb of a city in the Pacific Northwest. Imagine I had made an appointment and gone to see my pastor to explain that my behaviors that reflect my borderline personality disorder have become much worse. Indeed, I was often unable to act within the bounds of what is socially acceptable for our congregation.

"It's not that I yell at anybody," I might have said, "I just speak my mind forcefully these days."

Now, imagine with me, the pastor answers, "Yes, I've heard about this. This is a human experience that people have. What we will need to do is educate the entire congregation about people who have a different kind of personality structure. We will train the whole congregation to recognize when you are acting in an unusual manner and teach them that you are not making a social error or *faux pas*. We will be sure to incorporate some hymns into our worship that emphasize the variety of personality structures amongst God's people so that you will feel welcome."

What does this imagined conversation between me and the pastor tell us about mental illness? I believe it is 50 years too soon for that conversation to occur. In 2017, when my behaviors motivated by mental illness became more pronounced, it was not the case that a pastor could be expected to know what type of human experience she was hearing me describe.

It was 50 years too soon to train an entire congregation to recognize the behaviors of someone with a different personality structure. It was 50 years too soon to incorporate some hymns about the delightful variety of human beings God has created which includes human beings with different personality structures.

In other words, I foresee this: in 50 years, the behaviors I exhibit will be seen as evidence that I am a certain kind of person, but we will have moved on in our understanding that there are more kinds of people than we thought there were. Persons with nonstandard personality structures will not be seen as mentally ill, but as persons with nonstandard personality structures.

Some people once thought that being the descendent of slaves meant that you were somehow defective. Some people once thought that being the mother of small children meant that you couldn't think very well or have a career. Some people once thought that feeling a romantic attraction to a same-sex person meant you were defective. Some people once thought that feeling you were not a girl when you had been identified as a girl at birth meant that you were bad or wrong.

I believe the day will come when people with my challenges are not seen as being defective. Certainly, there are challenges in life from the things that I am facing. We know there are some challenges for some people who had ancestors that came here as slaves. Clearly, there are challenges for a female adult person who wants to nurture small children and pursue a career. But challenges do not imply defect.

Why Use the DSM?

I will soon be citing the DSM, the American Psychiatric Association's encyclopedic *The Diagnostic and Statistical Manual of Mental Disorders*; it contains descriptions of human behavior and symptoms of human problems in the area of mental disorders. Along with these, it contains criteria for diagnosing these mental disorders.

The DSM was never intended to be a weapon to beat people down. It is intended for diagnosis. Diagnoses can be used, and diagnoses can be misused. This is true of diagnoses in the area of mental illness and diagnoses in other areas.

For example, a diagnosis could be misused if it is treated as a label that limits a person. Suppose you receive a diagnosis of hypertension, that is, high blood pressure. Possibly a physician might tell you to avoid eating a lot of salt. It could be considered a misuse of that diagnosis — assuming the diagnosis is a label — if you orient your life from that moment onward around salt. Imagine you become the NaCl person on your block. The first thing you tell someone after you tell them your name is that you have hypertension and you eat no salt at all, ever. You become distressed when you find out that the potatoes you buy at the store have some naturally occurring salt inside their very structure. Here would be an example of using a diagnosis as a label, as a limit. Rather than giving helpful information, the diagnosis gave limitations and distortion to a human life.

The DSM is misused if a diagnosis is given and then the diagnosis is received by a patient or a patient's family or some healthcare professional and applied in a manner that limits a human life or distorts the capabilities of some human person. It is never my intention in my writing to suggest that anything in the DSM is meant to limit what some human beings can do or will do or have done. Nothing in the DSM should ever be taken to mean that some human person has no capacity to move beyond, through, or past any of the challenges that may be present in their life at some moment in time.

Any description of any human behavior or thought process or life pattern that may be written in this book could be present in any person at some moment in their life, but that would not necessarily be significant to a trained professional who is using the DSM to draw conclusions. Be careful. Recognizing in these pages some behavior or attitude in yourself or in someone you care about may not have any meaning. If you have any concerns, ask around amongst your friends and colleagues to find a respected and well-established healthcare professional. Ask that person your questions. If you have no money to hire someone, your county mental health department almost certainly has that service for free.

In 50 years from now, I think, there will be no DSM. I believe our conception of mental illness will have developed to the point where we understand it differently. Just as we are learning that adult-onset diabetes is not just one illness, but a number of physical processes that present at some point as high blood sugar, I think we will learn that mental illness is best understood in many more categories than we are aware of today. Current research is progressing at a rapid rate and the future looks bright.

CHAPTER 4
Borderline Diagnosis: DSM-IV and DSM-5

IN JUNE OF 2011, the American Psychiatric Association revised its published criteria for the diagnosis of Borderline Personality Disorder (BPD), as it replaced its DSM-IV manual with the DSM-5. The former, more succinct, criteria are more appropriate for the purposes of this book, however. I quote: *BPD is a pervasive pattern of instability in interpersonal relationships, self-image, and emotion, as well as marked impulsivity beginning by early adulthood and present in a variety of contexts, as indicated by **five (or more)** of the following:*

1. *Frantic efforts to avoid real or imagined abandonment. Note: Do not include suicidal or self-mutilating behavior covered in Criterion 5.*
2. *A pattern of unstable and intense interpersonal relationships characterized by alternating between extremes of idealization and devaluation.*
3. *Identity disturbance: markedly and persistently unstable self-image or sense of self.*
4. *Impulsivity in at least two areas that are potentially self-damaging (e.g., spending, sex, substance abuse, reckless driving, binge eating). Note: Do not include suicidal or self-mutilating behavior covered in Criterion 5.*

5. *Recurrent suicidal behavior, gestures, or threats, or self-mutilating behavior.*
6. *Affective instability due to a marked reactivity of mood (e.g., intense episodic dysphoria, irritability, or anxiety usually lasting a few hours and only rarely more than a few days).*
7. *Chronic feelings of emptiness.*
8. *Inappropriate, intense anger or difficulty controlling anger (e.g., frequent displays of temper, constant anger, recurrent physical fights).*
9. *Transient, stress-related paranoid ideation or severe dissociative symptoms.*

CHAPTER 5

Abandonment Fears

Frantic efforts to avoid real or imagined abandonment. Note: Do not include suicidal or self-mutilating behavior covered in Criterion 5. (DSM-IV)

LET'S DISCUSS ABANDONMENT issues, the part of the DSM diagnostic criteria listed here at the beginning of Chapter 5. Children who end up having borderline personality disorder experience profound abandonment in childhood. But it does not mean that their parents literally, that is physically, leave them. Suzy and Bill were simply emotionally unavailable to me.

Suzy and Bill were not emotionally prepared to be parents. They did not have adequate emotional resources to meet their own needs, much less each other's needs. When their babies were born, these parents were probably looking for a source of emotional support, rather than understanding that they would need to provide emotional support to these new little humans.

Many mothers and fathers look to their little children for emotional support. Sometimes, it seems to work. Some children can be molded to be bright and cheerful and tell Mom and Dad every day how wonderful they are. My sisters and I were required to tell Suzy what a fine mother she was.

The horror of being abandoned while your parents are in plain view is that you can reach adulthood without knowing that you were abandoned. Many people go to their graves without the knowledge that they were emotionally deprived as children. Without the knowledge that you did not receive adequate emotional care, it is difficult to recover (though not impossible).

Fear of abandonment manifests in adults with borderline personality disorder in many different ways. Of course, it is different in different people. For me, it has been a major influence in the communications area of email and telephone calls.

If I send someone an email and I don't hear back from them within a day or two, I am certain that they dislike me. For example, I recently sent an email to someone who works with me in a volunteer organization, asking her if she would manipulate a spreadsheet so that the information was sorted according to what street the people live on. When I didn't hear back from her in two days, I began to consider that she might be annoyed with me for asking her for too many favors. I wondered if a third person whom we both know had told her something bad about me. I wondered if I had been offensive the last time I spoke to her. I worried.

Although my thinking mind was able to interject thoughts about the possibility that she was busy or ill or that she was happy to do it and she would do it soon, the part of me that has borderline personality disorder now feels some kind of shame and is certain that I am broken and I am being rejected. This hurts so much that it overwhelms my thinking mind. My thinking mind is still talking to me, but it does not make any difference.

On the other side of the coin, if someone sends me an email, I feel an extreme urgency to answer right away for fear that they will feel rejected. I have an exaggerated sense of my own power because I imagine that if I don't answer, I will have a huge impact on their life. This is a terrible burden. Even while my thinking mind is telling me that this person does not suffer from borderline personality disorder, I am compelled to answer the email as soon as possible.

For some reason I do not know, I am able to watch myself as I experience the symptoms and behaviors of borderline personality disorder. I have a very good analytical mind. It is a strange sensation to observe myself behaving in a manner that is motivated by mental illness and experiencing feelings that are motivated by mental illness, yet at the same time know that my thinking mind has no influence over the mental illness and cannot stop it in any way.

Being smart and knowing a lot about mental illness does nothing to help one overcome mental illness. One cannot think her way out of mental illness. No amount of knowledge or intelligence will rescue me from having borderline personality disorder.

As a caveat, I should say that it is certainly not desirable to be mentally ill and to know nothing about the challenges one is facing. I would say, in general, most challenges in life are easier to face if you know more about them. My point is only this: reading up on diabetes does not lower your blood sugar; learning all about borderline personality disorder does not stop you from having borderline personality disorder.

Lastly, fear of abandonment may have caused me to stay in my marriage for too long. Although I do not think divorce is ever a good thing, sometimes it is the best of the bad choices. I chose to marry someone who has the diagnosis we used to call "Asperger's syndrome."

He experiences very little compassion and no remorse. He does not connect with human beings very much at all.

When we met in 1982, neither of us understood that we had any kind of mental illness. Now, 38 years later, I can see that I chose someone who was not able to respond to my needs. I grew up in a family where no one responded to my needs, so that was familiar — it felt normal. However, I have been getting well. I no longer tolerate unkindness the way I once did.

But I had promised not to abandon this person. I knew what it was like to be abandoned, and I was determined not to do that to someone else. I was not going to be someone who just walked away. Unfortunately, the influence of the Christian church has sometimes reinforced that way of thinking. My mother stayed with my father, a Christian minister, through a 17-year marriage during which he beat her. (And toward the end, she beat him, also.) My determination not to be a person who abandons someone else clouded my ability to see that I, too, am a child of God and should be treated well.

Abandonment issues are complex. I have only touched upon them here. If questions arise from what I have written, any competent counselor or therapist will be able to provide guidance.

But guidance will not provide a cure.

CHAPTER 6
More Insight Into the Person Suzy

HOW DID SUZY come to be a person who could not want what was best for her daughters?

Let me say, first, that Suzy did not fail to want what was good for me 100% of the time. She did not fail to want what was good for me in every area of life. For example, I remember lying in a hospital bed when I was 14 years old, subsequent to a medical test. Suzy and Bill were both present, as was the doctor. The doctor adjusted or moved something as part of explaining to my parents what the invasive test had shown (I was bleeding substantially). When I cried out in pain, Suzy intervened and told the doctor, "She is really feeling pain — she doesn't complain unless it really hurts."

Suzy was not only speaking out to protect me but indicating that she had observed that I was not inclined to be wimpy about pain. So, she *could* act in my best interest and she *could*, at times, pull up from some part of herself a little knowledge of the kind of person I was. It is worthy of note that I remember this incident distinctly. I remember it because it was so unusual to have Suzy do something beneficial to me. It was unusual to have Suzy do something that revealed that she knew something about me.

Of course, Suzy provided food and medical care adequate for my survival. Not all parents do even this. I realize it is shocking to many people to hear me express the following sentiment; nonetheless, I have to say that Suzy did most of the things that allowed me to survive to adulthood, but did them in order to meet her need to appear to the world to be a good mother. She did not actually grasp the fact that there is a difference between putting on a show of being a good mother and truly wanting to be a good mother.

Suzy had been damaged so badly by her family of origin that she did not know that acting like a good mother was different than being a good mother. She did not know that imitating the behaviors of some neighbor who wants what is best for a child was different than wanting what is best for your child.

Suzy was raised in significant poverty. Suzy was raised in generational poverty that was not just a lack of money; it was a way of looking at the world and a way of thinking about life's possibilities and a way of viewing humanity. However, she did something that none of her four siblings did: she decided to move out of that subculture and into middle-class America. And she was spectacularly successful with her goal.

Here is the defining story of Suzy's life: When Suzy was quite young, my recollection is that she told me it was when she was six years old, she was at a friend's house and she was jumping on the couch. Her friend's mother came into the room and, seeing Suzy jumping on the couch, said, "Oh, let's not jump on the couch."

In a flash, Suzy understood that some families were different than her family. In her family, gentle words would not have been used to correct a child's misbehaving. In her family, possessions were not carefully selected and carefully preserved so that the home was clean and comfortable. Suzy could not articulate what she understood that day. In her

27

telling of the story, she went on to say that she decided at that moment that she was not going to continue to be like her family but was going to grow up to be like this other family. She saw at that moment that there was a different way of being in the world and she decided she was not going to follow in the footsteps of the family she had been born into.

Suzy was the most amazingly not-self-reflective person I have ever met. Her lack of ability to reflect upon any behavior or attribute of herself was a protective mechanism that was essential for her because she had no resources to face the horrors that were the realities of her life. For that reason, she could not reflect upon the significance of the story. She could not articulate what she had understood that day.

Suzy had understood, in a flash, that her primary allegiance was not going to be to her family of origin. To use Christian theological language: the Holy Spirit had come to her and called her to be something better and different. She had heard the call. Suzy wanted to live a life that was not a continuation of the damaging aspects of the surroundings she was daily submerged in.

From that moment on, Suzy's story told me, she knew that she was going to identify not with her family but with some other subculture of the culture surrounding her.

By the time I knew her, her goal had clearly become to move into the middle class and to maintain behaviors that demonstrated to herself and to everyone that she was not a poor person, not a fat person, not an uneducated person, not an impolite person, not a prejudiced person, not an insensitive person, not a person lacking in compassion, not an ugly person, not a stupid person, but rather, she was the perfect hostess, the perfect housekeeper, the perfect gardener, the perfect volunteer, and the perfect mother. (Let me add that her need to be perfect and her need to prove she was perfect did not, in my opinion, reflect perfectly what the Holy Spirit was calling her to be that day when she was six years old. However, orthodox Christian theology tells us that none of us gets it perfectly right when we strive to follow the voice of God.)

Suzy was extremely, extremely, outrageously intelligent. She brought her powerful intelligence to these particular goals in part because she had been denied the opportunity to bring her intelligence to other goals. In public school, she had been disallowed to study chemistry or physics. She was a girl, and it was the 1940s. In college, female students were still being told that they should study to become either a nurse or a teacher. Suzy had already done amazing things just to have accomplished graduation from high school and entrance into college. Her family of origin did not especially value education.

To require that she should also have fought to be allowed to be a scientist was asking too much. She was in an oppressed group, and she was successfully oppressed. Her intelligence was channeled into acceptable, so-called "feminine" pursuits. It was not good.

What is unusual about Suzy, in my opinion, is that she did not pretend to be the perfect hostess only when people were watching. She was not putting on a show. She was unaware that surfaces were not reality. After her guests had left, she might say to me, "People are so funny! Look! Jane brought chocolates to the party. My invitation said that people should not bring anything, and Jane knows that I don't eat candy." Because the comment began with an exclamation that indicated that Suzy thought people were funny, in her mind Suzy was assured that she was only amused by the behavior of Jane. Suzy believed that if she said she was amused by Jane bringing chocolates, then she was amused. Suzy believed that she could not be angry or resentful about the chocolates if she opened her mouth and said that it was amusing.

29

She believed that the surface was the reality.

Imagine how it was for me, a child who was five years old or six years old living with a mother who was angry every minute of every day. This angry Suzy was using an angry voice to say, "Pick up that game and put it in the cupboard. The reason we have that cupboard with doors is so that I don't have to look at your games. I don't mind you having toys; I just don't want to have to see them."

The child apologizes for making Suzy angry and then finds out that she is in even more trouble. "I'm not angry!"

In Suzy's mind, a good mother was never angry with her children. So, little Jansen was broken. Little Jansen was wrong and broken to suggest that Suzy was angry. When a parent consistently tells a child that their reality is not reality, the child adjusts by believing that they are mistaken. It is crazy-making. This is the way that Suzy created mental illness in me. This is the actual process.

Suzy modified reality whenever it was convenient for her. But I'll come back to that later.

Still, I haven't explained how Suzy herself was so badly damaged. First, her parents did not take care of her. Suzy told a story about falling off a porch when she was six years old. Her arm did not break — it bent. She had rickets so badly that her arm could not break. Rickets is a disease of malnutrition. She was taken to the doctor and she remembers the doctor telling her parents that she was to be given meals three times a day. Again, Suzy would tell that story without any interpretation or conclusion. My own conclusion is that her parents had not been feeding her adequately. They were poor, but not so poor that they were not, themselves, getting enough food.

(Trigger alert: the following two paragraphs describe child abuse.)

Suzy was tied up with ropes when it was inconvenient for her mother to watch over her. She was locked in a closet. Like other children, she was sent to select some hard piece of vegetation with which to be beaten. I heard no stories from Suzy about anything that happened to her in childhood that reflected any kindness or caring. I heard no stories from Suzy about receiving an appropriate gift from her parents that was memorable. I never heard a story about a favorite toy or piece of clothing. The only stories Suzy told about her family of origin that had any positive quality were about her father's cheerfulness and fortitude when facing inadequate funds and food.

Suzy told me several times that her father bought her inappropriate clothing. He bought her high heel shoes when she was much too young, she said. He bought her silk stockings when she was quite young, she told me. Suzy was not protected from the neighbor. She was the oldest of five children, and she changed the diapers of the younger children, I was told. I would assume she did a great deal of other household labor.

Suzy grew up in a home that had no love. Her parents had not married for love. My maternal grandmother, Ruth, told me that she herself had been married off at 16 because her mother did not want to have her around. When my child was born, I went with my babe to see Ruth, thinking I was doing something kind. Ruth would not consent to hold her great-grandson. She said that she was not very good with babies and her mother had never allowed her to hold her own babies.

Here one can see the generational nature of early childhood trauma. But also, one can see that Suzy really wanted to do something better than that which was done to her.

Suzy had a deep conviction that she wanted to avoid the mistakes made

31

by her parents. Unfortunately, her understanding of the mistakes made by her parents extended only to poverty and physical violence. Suzy could see that it would be better for her children to live in the middle class. Suzy could see that it would be better if her children were not tied up or locked in closets.

However, for Suzy to face the deeper implications of the horror of what was done to her was simply more than she could handle. I wonder if it would have killed her. Her defense was denial. Denial is not always a mistake. If staying alive under such conditions is a good thing, then denial worked for Suzy.

Suzy did provide a middle-class home. She did not avoid physical violence against her children. But she reduced it from the very blatant violence that she experienced to the merely blatant violence against my older sister and violence masked as other behaviors against myself and my younger sister. Is that better?

There is a heroic aspect to Suzy's life. After high school, she was working for a dentist and, being the very intelligent person she was, she asked him so many technical questions that he lent her a textbook one evening. The next day, she returned to her job having read a substantial amount of the book. She had many more questions. The man recognized her abilities and arranged for her to go to college.

Her time at a nearby Lutheran college (now called a university) was funded by the people who make Almond Roca candy. Another story Suzy often told was a story about going to eat at the home of these people whom she perceived as very fancy people. This inspired her to read etiquette books.

She told a story of encountering an egg in an egg cup and having no idea what to do. She watched carefully to see what the hostess did and imitated that behavior. (I was trained according to the etiquette books with all of the manners she imagined I would need to marry into, um, I don't know, the Kennedy family? The British royal family? The Obama family?)

I don't know why she did not finish her degree at that first college, but I do know she was teaching school on Washington's Olympic Penninsula, in a rough neighborhood. She told me that one little boy in the kindergarten class became distressed one day. He hid under his desk and brandished a knife. He was taken away and never returned.

After that job, she married and found herself in Columbus, Ohio, where Bill was in seminary studying to be a Lutheran minister. She enrolled in a local college even though it was scandalous for a married woman to be insisting on finishing her degree. Why would she need a degree, after all, since she was already married? And then she conceived a child!

There was a meeting of the dean of students with some administrator to determine whether her request to be allowed to stay in school would be granted. My sister's birthday is in June, so Suzy's graduation took place when she was visibly pregnant. She did not fight to be allowed to take physics in high school, but this she did fight about — and she walked to get her diploma while looking very big.

When Bill was done with seminary, he wanted to accept a call to a country in South America to start a mission church. My older sister, then three years old, would have been separated from Suzy and put in a residential school. Suzy would not consent. As she told the story, "I asked them who would wash my little girl's hair since there was no live-in adult helper for the children. They told me that the children helped each other." Bill was very angry that Suzy would not go with him to South America.

So, Bill and Suzy and their first daughter went to Canada to establish a church. I was born there, as was my younger sister. Bill was paid $200 per month. Bill had begun to beat Suzy from the beginning of their marriage. In fact, stories she told me about physical unkindness that began before they had married leave no doubt that these were two horribly damaged people.

Like many women suffering abuse, Suzy left Bill repeatedly before she left him successfully. She announced she was moving back to the United States in 1965. He chose to come with her. He left the ministry at that time.

She went back to school.

She told him to get out of her home in 1974. The loss of a job forced her to move with her two younger daughters to another state, and that is where I finished high school.

She worked as a school psychologist from the time she finished graduate school until her retirement in 1994. Then she moved to my city to be near me and her grandson, my son.

Suzy liked being the grandmother who showed up with toys and candy. She liked being the grandmother who took my son out to do fun things. But when my son got to be old enough to assert himself as a human being — old enough to push back against what Grandma wanted to do or complain about the gift she had brought, she was no longer interested in a relationship with him. Suzy was capable of a happy relationship only with someone who would worship her. She could not engage in adult relationships, that is, relationships that involved some give-and-take.

Suzy remained friends with one person from the neighborhood I grew up in. However, I think I was the person most consistently emotionally close to her in her life. Maybe not. In any case, she lived within three miles of me until her death in 2013 at age 81. At the end, she had come to be so angry and bitter toward her children that she had removed all the pictures of her children and grandchildren from the walls of her home and replaced them with pictures of her dogs. She had changed her advanced medical directive so that her daughters could not make decisions about her medical care at the end of her life. As a result, my younger sister and I stood clutching each other and weeping in her hospital room as she suffered on the day she died. Her brother, whom she had named as the person who could authorize more pain medication, was not present and had turned off his phone, even though he knew his sister was dying.

It was her daughters who were there. But she did not trust us. She had no ability to understand human beings. She often said to me, "Everyone who was supposed to love me has betrayed me." This she said right to my face — and more than once. She was not a kind and caring person. She did not understand why she had the perception that she was being betrayed. She considered it a betrayal if I did not come to her house for dinner when invited. Indeed, there was no way to avoid giving Suzy the impression that she was being betrayed. She was angry all the time, and she felt betrayed by everything.

There was no way to be kind to Suzy. One never succeeded at pleasing Suzy.

Suzy did not know that she was in emotional pain. The reality that she was enduring psychological suffering was something she could not admit into her world. Being unable to be aware that she had any troubles to face, she was a person who never made any progress. It was profoundly sad.

Her suffering just went on and on and on. There was simply nothing anyone could do.

It was so sad, such a waste of a life.

CHAPTER 7
Unstable, Intense Relationships

A pattern of unstable and intense interpersonal relationships characterized by alternating between extremes of idealization and devaluation. (DSM-IV)

THE DSM CRITERIA for borderline personality disorder call out a pattern of unstable relationships with human beings. Does this apply to me?

First, I want to ask a different question: how did I survive? How did I come to be 60 years old, newly divorced after being married 33 years, the owner of a very nice home in the suburbs of a city and retired from a 20-year career teaching math and computer science at local colleges?

I am surprisingly successful, in the traditional measures of success, for a person with borderline personality disorder at the level of severity at which I am afflicted. Indeed, my diagnosis was delayed for three decades because most people who are as ill as I am cannot dress in clean clothing, sit in a doctor's office, and converse with a doctor.

When I was in treatment at the very best dialectical behavioral therapy

(DBT) treatment facility in my area, my therapist there said to me, "With all the things you are facing, I'm amazed that you don't live under a bridge." She meant that a person with my kind of suffering does not usually have the ability to live in a house. They do not have the skills to conduct themselves in such a manner that they can have an income and pay rent (much less pay a mortgage) and take care of the many things one needs to do to have stable housing.

Without stable housing, the challenges of having a clean body and clean clothes are often beyond those who are suffering the way I suffer. When my PTSD is added to my borderline troubles, and then added to the diagnosed depression, and then added to the diagnosed anxiety, it is absolutely amazing that I do not live outdoors every day.

Let me tell you how I came to be in the happy position I'm in:

Suzy trained me to behave as if everything was fine 24/7. Of course, many troubled families teach their children to act as if everything is fine the moment they step out the front door. Many troubled families want the outside world to think that everything is fine. However, Suzy was a special case. Suzy was so damaged herself that she did not know the difference between surfaces and reality. In fact, she thought surfaces *were* reality. So, she taught me and my two sisters to imitate a normal family even when we were inside our own home. We acted like a not-chaotic family all day, every day.

Here's an example: I was taught to open my birthday gift from Suzy, put a smile on my face, look her in the eye and say, "Thank you, Mommy! This is really cool! This is just what I wanted!" It was not acceptable to call her "Mom," as that was against the rules. It was not acceptable for the smile to look fake; that was against the rules. The crazy-making part was that Suzy believed that a girl who opened a gift and smiled in just the right way and said the correct words *actually liked the gift*.

Suzy did not know that it was possible for a child to dislike a gift that she had purchased for that child if she could get the child to put the correct expression on her face and say the correct words. Suzy thought the surface was the reality.

If a parent does not know that a child has inner experience, then they do not make any attempt to discern the child's actual inner experience. A child who grows up having her inner experience consistently discounted, completely ignored, does not know that she has inner experience. She thinks that Suzy dictates her experience. It makes her, um, crazy.

This bizarre version of "how the world really is," which I absorbed as a child, has been problematic. I'm sure you can imagine how that would be so. But it has had a strange benefit to me. Because Suzy taught me to behave as if everything were fine — all day, every day — I emerged into adulthood with a complete set of skills to carry on an adult life.

Thus, I completed high school. I went to college for two years at an East Coast university and then finished up in two years at a Lutheran college. I spent two years in graduate school but decided not to finish that degree. I started a business and supported myself cleaning houses in a city in the Pacific Northwest. Then I moved to the city I live in now, and I married.

Throughout my 20s and 30s and 40s, I was acutely aware that something was not right in my life. Both of my parents were still living, and I was communicating with both of them. I had a growing awareness that my family of origin had been significantly troubled. I had my two insightful and intelligent sisters to help me know that the very odd things I recalled from childhood were real. But I had no idea that I was merely imitating normal life.

I owe thanks to Suzy for training me in 100 skills that have allowed me to stay alive. Suzy was a survivor. She, herself, figured out how to get an education. When she announced to husband Bill that she was moving, with her daughters, back to the United States, and he could come along if he chose, she did move. And she immediately began graduate school. Then she got a job as a school psychologist. As soon as she could support her family, she told him to leave her home. She was a survivor.

Suzy also instilled in me a belief that God wins in the end. To say that differently, because I do not feel a need to use Christian language exclusively, Suzy lived knowing that what is real in this universe has a benevolent twist and is not indifferent to human beings. Bill, also, lived from that reality. As horrible as my parents were, they both were people who believed that ultimately good is more powerful than evil — which is true.

The story of how I came to understand that I was imitating normal life, that I was not experiencing normal life in any genuine manner, I will leave for the next chapter.

That is how I survived: I survived by living a life that had nothing to do with Jansen. I was a robot who was imitating normal life. I did the things I had been taught to do. I had no idea what I wanted to do, only what I had been told I would want to do. I did not have fun; I only laughed when I knew I was supposed to laugh. I did not enjoy the sunset; I only said the things I knew I was supposed to say when I saw a sunset. But, having no frame of reference, I thought I was having fun and I thought I was enjoying a sunset.

This brings me to the subject of this chapter, which is unstable relationships with people. Perhaps you can guess that I am going to say I did not have unstable relationships with people! During the part of my life when I was in this deep state of freeze, living a life I had been trained to live that was unrelated to anything real in myself, I had very stable relationships. They were stable because they were not relationships based on anything real about me.

In this manner, I was able to be married for 33 years. I was able to be a member of a church for 33 years. I lived in the same house all of the years I was raising my son. I was quite successful at raising my son. And, to continue to comment on a stable life that is unlike the usual life of someone as ill as I am, I am not addicted to any substance; I do not gamble away my money; I have had no suicide attempts; I have no self-harm habits that require medical attention; I do not yell at people and swear at them; I don't shoot people or find myself in situations where I get shot at; that is, I have a very calm life, unlike many people suffering from borderline personality disorder with my level of severity.

When my son was two years old, I selected a local daycare service. He was there four days a week for five hours a day. This allowed me to resume my main entertainment, which was taking one class each term at the local State University. Before his birth, I had been taking math classes for fun. When he was two, I decided to entertain myself by taking computer science classes.

I started with the course, "Introduction to Programming." It was 1990, and we were programming in Pascal. I finished the basic 100-level courses and was in the midst of the more advanced 200-level series of theoretical courses (discrete math, symbolic logic, theory of computation) when I decided to apply to the graduate school to earn a master's degree in computer science.

I was not accepted, but the chair of the department stopped me in the hall to tell me that the rejection was only because I had not finished the three theory courses at the 200 level.

I did not bother to reapply for the master's program but continued taking one class each term for my own amusement. The most valuable part of taking a class, for me, is that paying tuition entitles me to go to the professor's office hours and speak to her or him one-on-one. One day I was talking to a professor who said, "The faculty has been discussing how to improve the quality of the master's degree students here at this school. What are your thoughts?"

"Well, I'm not one of the graduate students," I told him.

He was surprised. He then replied, telling me that I always wrote exactly the right program on the exams (it was a class in functional and declarative programming languages). Then he told me that he would like me to apply to the master's degree program immediately. He would arrange for me to be accepted. He would hire me to be his research assistant, so I would be paid to go to school. When I told him that I was not sure I wanted to take a full load of classes, he explained that he could invent some fake classes so that I appeared to have a full load even though I did not.

This is how I came to be in graduate school again. This did not happen by accident. This happened because I have learned to behave as if I am just as important in this world as anyone else. Having been raised in a family in which my needs were hardly ever important, I have learned to assert myself in situations where I can see that I will get something I want. An advantage I have over many people who are struggling with borderline characteristics is that I usually can assert myself without transgressing the boundaries of other people. And I often get what I want — sometimes I get even more than I had hoped for!

In a way, it is sad that my very low self-esteem forces me to behave *as if I am just as important in this world as anyone else.* There is no part of me, at least no part that I am aware of today, that thinks I am just as important as anyone else. When a little infant is treated as if she is a problem, not a person, and that treatment persists while she is a toddler, then a small child, and then a big kid and a teenager, it is not easily overcome. (And let me say again that neither Suzy nor Bill had any intention of mistreating me. They were not aware that they were treating me as if I was a problem. They were both badly damaged people themselves And the horror of my family of origin was an emergent property, not anything planned by anyone.)

Some little hints of who the real Jansen might be occasionally peeked through. After all, for entertainment, I did take classes at the local State University. That is something the genuine Jansen would do (if you will excuse my speaking about myself in the third person). For entertainment, someone else might take up knitting or scuba diving. And the subject of my studies was math and computer science, not French literature. Again, that reflects the real Jansen.

Yet, I know very little about who I am, even today at age 60. Neither of my parents had any interest in knowing who their daughter was. They were not aware that getting to know one's child was even a possibility. I married a person who does not fully grasp the presence in the world of other human beings. He has told me that if a person is not physically present and visible in front of his face, he has a limited ability to think about them or recall their presence in the world. Marrying him was an unfortunate choice, in a way, but it meant that, initially, I had a husband who treated me the way I was already accustomed to being treated.

I am not entirely convinced that there is some real Jansen underneath all of these behaviors that I was taught. But I am looking for clues. Looking for clues at age 60 is strange indeed!

CHAPTER 8
Unstable Sense of Self

Identity disturbance: markedly and persistently unstable self-image or sense of self. (DSM-IV)

HOW DID I find out that I was imitating normal life rather than living the life of some real Jansen?

Here is the story of how that happened: I was in treatment at a DBT clinic in my city. DBT is dialectical behavioral therapy, a therapy for treating some of the symptoms of borderline personality disorder. DBT was created by Marsha Linehan of the University of Washington. It addresses the problems faced by persons struggling with borderline personality disorder that are created when they become distressed and take action to relieve their distress in the short term — often quite successfully relieving their distress in the short term — but create for themselves big problems in the long term.

This was not just any clinic delivering dialectical behavioral therapy. This DBT clinic is staffed by especially highly-qualified therapists and professionals. Quite a few of them have earned PhDs studying directly with Marsha Linehan. They really know what they're talking about.

(This stands in contrast to the DBT implementations I had been exposed to at my HMO which were led by people who had had only a two-day training.)

One day in 2015, I was sitting in a DBT group session. The state of DBT at that time was such that the four DBT modules were always taught with the same group exercises. I had been in DBT groups through my HMO for quite a few years, and I had been at this DBT clinic for a couple of years. So, the group exercise we were doing that day was one I had done about 10 or 11 times before. At the end of the exercise, the group leader always says, "Now, make note of this relaxed feeling so that you can access it in the future when you need it."

On the 11 previous occasions that I had done this exercise, I had thought, "I must not be good at making note of the relaxed feeling I am having." This thought had gone through my mind because I could not access any relaxed feeling. However, on this occasion, I thought, "Perhaps I do not have a relaxed feeling!"

I mentioned this to my therapist (DBT treatment involves both group work and individual therapy) at my weekly session, and she was perceptive enough to ask me some questions about the variety of inner experience I was able to report. Together we discovered that I was not able to report any inner experience that varied from day to day or from hour to hour or from minute to minute.

To give you an example, she asked me if I experienced anger as a sensation more in my chest or in my gut. I was baffled. I did not know what the question meant. She tried to explain what it meant to have a sensation in one's chest. I could not understand the meaning of her words. We came to understand that I do not have any sensations in my chest.

I have been assured by every therapist I have ever had that I have emotions. To be a human being is to have emotions. I observed that I will begin to weep in some situations. Certain kinds of jokes cause me to laugh. But I have no sensations in my body that correspond to emotions — at least none that I can access.

This fine therapist had helped me learn something no one else had helped me learn: I am numb inside. Many were the psychiatrists who had asked me if I felt empty inside or numb inside. Of course, I had answered no. Psychiatrists have some standard questions that they ask; this is one of them. It is meant to determine if a person has become depressed. When a person becomes extremely depressed, she often feels empty inside or numb inside.

The question about feeling hollow or empty is not meant to identify people who have had no connection to their bodies for their entire life. I had mentioned some of the symptoms of being radically disconnected from my body to various mental health professionals over the years, but none of them had picked up on the importance of my words until I came across this especially attuned therapist at the DBT clinic.

(When I was a student at that East Coast university, I had gone to the student health department and said that I needed to see a psychiatrist. I had asked to be evaluated because of some symptoms I was describing; this, in hindsight, was my attempt to say that I was in a state of complete dissociation. I was evaluated for a dissociative disorder. It was determined that I do not have a dissociative disorder, and I believe this is true.)

So, that is the story of how I came to understand that other people see a flowering tree in the springtime and have some inner experience of pleasure which causes them to say, "What a beautiful tree!" But I had always commented on the beautiful tree in the springtime because I believed that it was a rule: it is spring; I see a flowering tree; I say that the tree is beautiful. I did not know that the motivation of other human beings was not a rule they learned from their mothers.

This brings me to the subject of this chapter that is the characteristic of many borderline sufferers: having an unstable sense of self. An unstable sense of self might cause a person to be quite certain that she likes to have several pets in the house and likes the mild chaos of living things all around her but then, the very next day, be quite certain that she likes a life optimized for maximal freedom so that she can jump on an airplane and go anywhere she wants at a moment's notice. These two conflict.

Naturally, every person has desires that conflict. The difference is that a borderline sufferer might be absolutely certain on Tuesday that having no pets is very important and absolutely certain on Wednesday that having pets is important. In contrast, someone whose sense of self is stable could recognize on Tuesday both wanting to have pets and wanting to have freedom. And on Wednesday, they would again recognize that they both want to have pets and want to have freedom.

It is this difficulty with holding two ideas that are in conflict in one's mind that creates a problem for many people with borderline personality disorder. This is part of the reason that Marsha Linehan came to understand that dialectics is a key to helping borderline sufferers. Black-and-white thinking — that is, thinking that things are completely in one category or completely in the opposite category — is characteristic of the thinking of people struggling with borderline personality disorder.

Dialectical thinking recognizes opposing forces, the simultaneous existence of conflicting ideas. So, to look at our previous example, a person who does not think in black-and-white terms is able to say, "I both want to have pets and want to be able to travel at the drop of a hat."

But a person who suffers from an inability to think in shades of gray or to hold two conflicting ideas in mind at once might think, "I can either want pets or I can want to travel, but not both."

Let me be clear: it is not that people who suffer from borderline personality disorder are lacking in intelligence. People who think in black-and-white terms are not bad thinkers. Many of them are very successful in the world of academia. The limitation comes from an inability to tolerate the discomfort of ambiguity or ambivalence. But I will address that in another chapter.

I am in the happy position of not having an unstable sense of self. I have no sense of self whatsoever. I know almost nothing about who I am. I don't know what foods I would eat if I chose the foods I like. I don't know what foods I like. No food tastes good to me except anything that is high in salt and sugar and fat, but that is true because the human body is hardwired to like salt and sugar and fat. Those are things that will keep us alive.

I don't know what kind of movies I like. The only movies I watch are the ones that are rated G. Any other movies trigger my PTSD. So, my movie choices are based on avoiding the experience of being overwhelmed by all of the trauma of a lifetime of being treated by the people who should have cared about me the most, as if I have no needs.

I don't know what kind of clothing I like. I don't like my curves to show because I don't like to have sexual attention from men — that attention is frightening to me. So, I wear clothing that is modest in the sense that Muslim women's clothing is modest.

Yet, one characteristic of borderline personality disorder can be a need for attention; I wear unusual clothing that gets attention for being artistic, lacy, colorful, color-coordinated from head to toe, feathery, old-fashioned, hand-painted and spectacular. But I don't know if I like that kind of clothing or if it simply is meeting a need.

I don't know what kind of people I like. I don't know what kind of music I like. Actually, I do not have inner experiences of pleasure, so I don't know anything about what I like.

I don't know how to go about establishing a sense of self without access to physical sensations. I'm not sure there can be any sense of self without having a body. Currently, I have almost no access to any information from my body, so I don't know much about myself.

I had been referred to the DBT clinic to be treated for self-harming behaviors that were not life-threatening. As I mentioned before, these are also self-harming behaviors that are so mild that they don't require medical attention. At the DBT clinic, they were not able to help me with that problem. After some years with them, I was advised to go on to pursue treatment for the difficulty I have with physical sensations.

I am happy to say that research in the area of healing the damage from trauma, especially very early childhood trauma, through therapies that address our physical bodies, is moving ahead by leaps and bounds. Although I have had challenges finding a competent therapist, it is now possible to find someone who is capable of helping me in my journey toward having access to physical sensations.

In this journey, I have lost my marriage and I have lost my family.

On my father's side, I have 17 cousins. Not one of them, as far as I know, has examined the kind of family patterns that are being handed down. I have never heard any discussion of our shared grandparents as people who were not able to nurture children. I have never heard any discussion of our aunts and uncles as people who unintentionally harmed their children the way Bill harmed his children.

On my mother's side, I have 17 cousins. There is one who, I heard indirectly, may know the truth. Otherwise, like my father's side of the family, these people are coping by maintaining their conviction that the family may have a few little troubles, but it's basically an okay family. The violence inflicted on all five of their children by our shared grandparents is not discussed. Even incidents that seem outrageous to me are treated as everyday events.

I am no longer able to be in contact with either of my sisters. My way of coping with the terrible abuse that I suffered is to look it squarely in the face and come to understand fully the damage that was done to me. One of my sisters copes mostly by using denial. Though denial has a bad reputation as a coping strategy in popular culture, it is actually a very important and powerful way to cope. I cannot be in a relationship with this sister because I have nothing to talk about except for my suffering. My suffering and my attempts to get well are the only activities of my life. I have nothing else to say in a conversation. Talking about these things would challenge her denial, and that would be harmful to her.

My other sister seems to have suffered some kind of crisis when our mother died. I am not sure what happened. However, there are some family patterns I no longer will repeat. One part of my break with this sister was that I declined to engage in a certain kind of conversation that was part of an old family pattern. I just wouldn't do it. Whether that was a problem for her or not, I do not know. Our mother died; my sister wanted to discuss a certain thing; I wouldn't do it; she cut off contact with me.

It is better, though, for me to spend some time away from my sisters. We did not have loving relationships. If we had had solid, loving relationships that were perturbed by a few problems, we could have worked on being better sisters to each other. But there was no love in our family. And I cannot establish loving relationships with human beings at this time. So much less am I likely to establish loving relationships with two women who also came from a family of horror.

I don't want to be misleading: my sisters have behaved toward me in a loving manner. Like me, they were trained by Suzy. Also, I believe neither of them was damaged as badly as I was by our family of origin. There are several reasons that I am doing less well than they are. They are kind people, and they have not harmed me.

I have had to leave behind all of those aunts and uncles and cousins, my husband, both of my sisters, three nieces, and a nephew. My son has chosen not to be in contact with me at this time.

It is sad.

Still, I hope the day will come when I will see my son again. I hope the day will come when I can re-establish relationships with my sisters. It may take many years for me to gain access to physical sensations and get to know who I am. It is a daunting task.

But what is the other choice? There is no other **real** choice. The other, false, choice is to distract myself with some hobby or distract myself by focusing on making a lot of money or throw myself into some volunteer work. I could stay in this state of suffering. That is not a real choice for me.

For me, the only viable choice is to press forward toward wholeness. To use Christian language: the spirit of God continues to call me onward; onward toward my full humanity, toward wholeness, toward being the person I was meant to be!

CHAPTER 9
More Insight Into the Person Bill

I KNOW A lot about Suzy because I was subjected to being her confidant in a most inappropriate manner. But I know quite a bit less about Bill as a person. I recall only two conversations in which he shared with me information about himself as a person.

In one of those conversations, I asked him about the violence he inflicted on my mother. It was summertime, and I was living in his home in the university district of a city in the Pacific Northwest.

As soon as Suzy had made Bill leave her home, Bill quit his job and started his own company putting up acoustical ceilings. That was in 1974 when I was 14 years old. During the summers of 1978 and 1979, I worked for Bill putting up acoustical ceilings as his employee. He permitted me to live in his home where he lived with his second wife, Sunny, whom he had married in 1975. Also living there were my older sister (still in school) and Sunny's only child, a daughter the same age as I.

I had asked him about his violent behavior as gently as I possibly could — not in a confronting manner. We were in the sunroom just off the kitchen and no one else was in the room. He talked about how vicious and mean Suzy was with her words. He talked about how deeply angry he could become when she attacked him with her words. He wept one or two tears as he described how angry he had felt. Then he talked about how he would devise angry speeches to deliver to her as he drove home from his construction job toward our house in the suburbs during the years that he still lived in a home with her. He talked about how his heart began to misbehave. He explained to me that during the subsequent tests on his heart, he was asked to exercise, and the monitor showed that his heart behaved better and better as he spent more time on the exercise bike.

This narrative was Bill's way of trying to tell me that even his body was beginning to suffer the consequences of the terrible stress of living with Suzy. The doctor concluded that the exercise was relieving stress, and his heart was beating normally as his body found an outlet for the pent-up anxiety.

Both of my parents were profoundly narcissistic. Bill gave me the best answer he could, and it was an answer that was completely Bill-centric: concerning the violence Bill had perpetrated against Suzy: it was anger, anger, stress, stress, suffering, suffering, me, me.

In a way, I cannot find fault with this response. Bill was, like Suzy, a terribly damaged person. If he had been capable of a less self-centered answer, he would have given a less self-centered answer. He simply was not able to reply in a manner that spontaneously spoke to the dynamic between himself and his wife or spoke at all to her suffering. The suffering of others was not a reality for Bill. In this, he matched Suzy.

Bill did not acknowledge that people had needs unless they were extremely obvious. When I was working for him, I was allowed to stop to attend to a physical need only if I was bleeding or vomiting. It was not acceptable for me or either of my sisters to stop working because we were thirsty or hungry or hot or tired. We could not stop to use the bathroom unless it was 10 a.m., the official break time. I recall one construction site on which the porta-potty had no door. I consulted my older sister about different ways we might create safety so that we could use the porta-potty (there were a number of other male construction workers on the site). I did not bother to ask Bill about this problem. He would not have perceived a problem. He would have said, "No one is going to hurt you." (I remember that I walked to a nearby swimming pool and used the toilet there.)

Bill was very casual about worker safety. During the summer of 1978, I was 5'6" tall and weighed 160 pounds. He was 5'11" tall and weighed about 200 pounds. He would load his pickup truck with acoustical ceiling tile cartons higher than the cab of the truck, adequately tied down, making the center of gravity of the load quite high. The brakes on the truck had not been properly maintained. To stop the loaded truck, Bill would put his right foot on the brake pedal and press with quite a bit of the weight of his body. For me to stop the truck, I had to put the entire weight of my body on the brake pedal. This was not safe. However, when I called this to Bill's attention, he declined to take any action regarding the brakes on the truck.

Bill was very casual about honesty. The money that I made working for him during the summer went toward my college tuition, room, and board. I had, of course, expenses such as books and fees, clothing, money needed for social events, money needed for church events and incidentals.

Every year I filled out the government forms so that I could borrow money from the federal government. I always qualified for the full amount of government loans. The federal government would specify how much each of my parents was to contribute to my education that year. Bill would make his contribution fraudulently as if I had worked more hours than I did. He would explain to me explicitly, "If I give you the money just as a gift, then I have to pay 50% tax on that money. In other words," Bill would say to me, "I have to make two dollars for every one dollar I give you because I am in the 50% tax bracket. But if I give you the money as if you worked more hours for me, then I don't have to pay as much tax on the money."

It was illegal and it was dishonest. (Also, that's not really what the 50% tax bracket means.) But what could I do? I was a starving student, and I did not feel I was in a position to object. Remember that this man was a Lutheran minister. He had started at age 27 to found a church in a suburban part of Canada. Presumably, he was following the way of Jesus, the Christ! Yet he was telling me his strategy for avoiding paying his fair share of taxes…with no shame.

Both Bill and Suzy were the oldest of five in their families of origin. Bill was born in Underwood, Minnesota. His father had been the only child of Helen and Pat Vee. Pat Vee had come over from Norway as a young adult, but his son, my grandfather, Sidney, was born in the United States.

Sidney, who went by "Sid," claimed to have no middle name. But there was a time when his mail got confused with some other Sid Vee. I wish I could understand how this happened, because I am related to every Vee in the United States. I haven't figured out how there could have been another "Sidney Vee." So, my grandfather began to go by "Sidney P. Vee." He consistently said that there was no particular reason that he had chosen a middle initial P. However, I learned to speak a little Norwegian and learned something about Norwegian names, and I asked him if it stood for "Patson." That would have been the traditional way to name him: Sidney, the son of Pat. Yes, he conceded, that was the reason he had chosen P.

Sid married my grandmother, Shay, and their son, Bill, was born in 1930. They had a herd of cows — I think they were dairy cows. Sometime around 1937, the cows had to be destroyed because of infection. Sid and Shay lost the farm; it reverted to the bank. Sid hopped on a train (yes, he actually rode a freight train) west to the high desert of Washington State, where he selected a new home for the family. This part I don't understand — did he buy some land?

So, when my father was seven years old, they packed up the family truck and drove to Washington State to start a new life.

The Vee family refers to this as *when the cows died*. There was considerable financial hardship after that, but that does not account for the kind of person Bill turned out to be. When one looks at Bill's emotional difficulties and the Vee family's patterns of behavior, it is not in the area of money troubles that one finds the roots of these gnarled trees. Shay suffered from tuberculosis a decade later, when the last two children were very small. All of the children were sent to various families to be cared for while she was in a sanatorium. This kind of life disruption is much more likely to produce people whose parenting is not-really-good-enough. But Bill would have been 12 or 13 years old, at least, by then.

No, the kinds of hardships that resulted in the difficulties that Bill had are exactly the kinds of hardships that Suzy faced. Bill, I am quite certain, was not tied up and locked in closets. But I know there was violence in the family. Once, when I was 32 years old and my son was four years old, I was at a Vee family gathering, and I spoke to Bill's youngest sister. I said to her, "You must have known that something was not right in the family when I was a little girl. Bill is a person who enforces his will with his fists. You must have known. Why didn't you come and rescue me?"

She answered, "We thought it was none of our business. Anyway, both of my adult children have had to sit in front of therapists to work through the trauma of the times that I hit them." She went on, "And I remember being sent out to choose a switch for beatings when I was a girl. And I deserved every one of those beatings." This was 1992, and the woman speaking to me was about 55 years old.

What does this say about the Vee family? This woman was in the Peace Corps in the 1960s or early 1970s. She was a young adult in college during a time of awakening — a time when we were thinking about peace and Vietnam and violence. Still, as the mother of adults, she had not thought through the beatings that she received as a child and realized that beating children is never okay. No child does anything that deserves a beating. My four-year-old was playing nearby. My four-year-old had no trouble understanding English words and English sentences. Right next to a four-year-old child, she is saying that she deserved to be beaten and, like Bill saying that he's going to cheat the government and saying it with no shame or self-consciousness, she is saying that she deserved to be beaten.

To comment further on the Vee family: when they hold a family reunion, the last thing they do is not something sweet — not something like holding a sentimental farewell ceremony or sending people off with special little handmade cards that say *until we meet again*. The last thing they do is read off a list of the people present and how many meals each person ate at the reunion gathering. Announced with each person's name and the number of meals they ate is the amount of money they owe for the food they consumed. I am not joking. No accommodation is made for the age of the person or their financial situation.

There is no softening of the delivery with any phrase such as, "If you can afford to contribute" or "Please give as much of the amount we're asking as you feel you can." Someone has been watching and making a tally of how many times you ate a meal at the family reunion!

From a family like this comes Bill, who would, occasionally, when visiting at my home announce, apropos of nothing, "It isn't good to help your children by giving them money. It makes them dependent and makes them weak." True to this sentiment, he refused to help me with money when I needed $1000 to pay the deductible on my health care insurance which I had, wisely, purchased when I was self-employed as a housecleaner in 1984. I had been hospitalized with a skin infection on January 1st and spent the thousand dollars in the first two days of the year. What a smart woman I was to purchase that health care insurance policy!

But, was I praised by my father? Did he tell me how I had been clever and used amazing foresight? No. He told me that helping me with money would make me weak. He refused.

Bill also announced, unprompted, on one visit, that he was giving away all of his money when he died, and I would not receive any inheritance from him. I am not sure why it was so important for him to tell me that. I was about 35 years old, and I had not planned my life around inheriting money from Bill. It is mystifying to me.

Bill's biggest fear in life was that his daughters would ask for something from him — especially that they would ask for money. When he died, his body was cremated. He had asked that his ashes be scattered over a certain island in the Strait of Juan de Fuca. My two sisters and I were in a small plane involved in a strange ceremony related to the scattering of his ashes, and my younger sister, with mischievous delight, suggested we throw coins out the window in addition to the dried flowers someone had provided (mistakenly thinking we wanted to do something nice for Bill). We tossed money out the window. We could not resist that symbolic gesture of truth-speaking. "This is the truth, Bill. In the end, the impression you left with your daughters was all about money. Here's what we think when we think about you: you really, really did not want to give us any money. You lived in fear that we would somehow get some money from you. You cared a lot about money. Here, have some money from me."

CHAPTER 10

Impulsivity

Impulsivity in at least two areas that are potentially self-damaging (e.g., spending, sex, substance abuse, reckless driving, binge eating). Note: Do not include suicidal or self-mutilating behavior covered in Criterion 5. (DSM-IV)

IMPULSIVITY IS ONE of the characteristics of borderline personality disorder because there are impulsive behaviors that can bring relief from some of the pain that people with this terrible illness are experiencing.

Have you ever noticed that there are people who do things that lead them to have miserable lives?

Though there are many reasons that people do things that lead them to have miserable lives, and borderline personality disorder is not always the reason, borderline personality disorder is sometimes the reason. Reckless gambling can bring some people relief, temporarily, from the pain they are experiencing. Having sex with strangers on a whim or even in a planned manner–for example, going to a bar to find a stranger as a partner, can bring temporary relief. Many impulsive behaviors can bring temporary relief from the pain. But in the long term, these behaviors can cause terrible problems.

One of the strangest things about my presentation of borderline personality disorder (to say "my presentation" is to say how I present myself to a doctor or other healthcare provider as a patient at an appointment) is that I do not have any impulsive behaviors that give me relief from pain in the short-term and make my life worse in the long term. This is extremely unusual.

In fact, my diagnosis was delayed for three decades because I was seeking mental health care while presenting in such an unusual manner. I showed up wearing clean clothing and did not smell like someone who had not bathed. I was on time for appointments and was able to sit in a room with a therapist or psychiatrist and speak calmly. I reported, truthfully, that I lived in a house and attended a church. I had a stable marriage and a stable income. I had successfully navigated high school and college. All of these are things that human beings suffering from borderline personality disorder at my level of severity do not normally do.

I want to make a comment here about persons who may have a diagnosis of borderline personality disorder but are not as severely afflicted as I am. It is quite common for those sufferers to be high-functioning. That is, it is not unusual for patients with a diagnosis of borderline personality disorder to live in a house and wear clean clothing and be successful physicians or attorneys and be successfully raising children.

My level of affliction is severe.

My affliction is so extreme that people like me normally receive health care and mental health care only when they are picked up by the police, involuntarily committed to a mental health care residential facility, or brought by ambulance to a hospital emergency department. It is not unusual for someone as ill as I am to arrive in an ambulance having been shot or otherwise attacked or suffering from some life-threatening problems related to living outdoors or having no stable housing.

It is emergency mental health practitioners who usually diagnose borderline personality disorder at the level of severity of mine. My diagnosis was delayed because therapists and psychiatrists who saw me in a setting where they were being paid by insurance policies associated with employers, not the state health plan, which mostly cares for people with much less money, saw a population of people who lived in houses and bathed regularly. Those people simply did not have the severe borderline illness I have, combined with my other diagnoses: PTSD, major depression without psychosis, generalized anxiety disorder, and binge eating disorder. Seeing patients who have upscale, top-drawer insurance policies guarantees that one's patient population will not be primarily persons as sick as I am.

For this reason, therapists completely missed the signs that I was severely ill and not simply someone with some depression. I recall, for example, seeing a therapist when I was in my early 30s. I distinctly remember telling her on several occasions that I felt terrible every day. She said to me, "Life is a mixed bag. Today you feel really down. Today you can't remember that on another day you felt good. So right now, you really believe that you feel bad every day. But life is a mixed bag. Some days you feel good, and some days you feel bad. You just can't remember, right now, that you have good days."

The therapist was not really hearing what I was saying, or she was hearing but not believing.

I was about 30 years old, and I was a severely mentally ill person. I was a person who did not have access to the feelings of my body. I had only the most tentative understanding of my own experience of life. I was desperately looking for help to understand what was happening to me.

So, I grasped at any straw. I believed her. I believed her. For at least 15 years, I told myself that I did have good days. Therapist X had taught me so. It must have been so. I must have had good days. I just couldn't remember them. That's what I said to myself, even though it was false.

If this woman had believed me when I said that I was miserable every day, she might have asked more questions and discovered that she was dealing with someone who was much more severely troubled than she thought. I might have gotten the correct diagnosis earlier. As it was, I did not receive the right diagnosis until I was past 50 years old. People seeing me in an office, while I was wearing clean clothing and talking about having food every day, did not ask themselves if they might be speaking to someone suffering at the level that I actually do suffer.

The disruptions that cause many borderline personality disorder sufferers to have chaotic lives, so chaotic that they cannot manage to keep their bodies and clothing clean, are often caused by impulsive behaviors that are unfortunately wildly successful temporary escapes from pain. I find it difficult to explain this to people who have not been in a state of pain that is so severe that they are willing to take action that will disrupt their lives for years to come to feel better for five minutes.

People will gamble and lose thousands of dollars in an afternoon. For that one afternoon, they will feel powerful. They will feel that they can do something effective in the world. They will feel they are somebody. They will feel they are important. Quite possibly the other people in the gambling establishment will be joking with them and enjoying their company. Maybe they will have a couple of drinks and be mildly intoxicated. They may be relaxed and happy-feeling. Three or four or five hours go by, and their life savings are gone. However, for those three or four or five hours, they were free of the horrible pain that comes from the abuse that brings about borderline personality disorder.

I understand them completely.

I know it is not the case that all human beings have suffered emotional pain to the same degree. Certainly, all people know what it is to have emotional pain. No one escapes the pain of loss. Everyone knows what it is to have a friend move to another city or have a beloved relative die or a beloved pet disappear mysteriously never to be seen again. Even a very young adult will have had some experience that allows them to understand loss — even if they are too young to have experienced the death of a beloved human friend or relation.

Everyone knows what it is to experience betrayal. No one escapes the horror of having someone they trust do something unimaginable. Even as children, we have this experience when our parents fail to be what we need them to be every moment of every day. By the time a young person is old enough to think in the abstract and articulate abstract thoughts, for most human beings about age 12 or 13, he or she can talk about disappointment and anger with another human being in some way that is recognizable. This is pain we all know.

I have always wanted to be careful not to claim that my suffering is somehow special. Having come from a Christian tradition, I have listened to many sermons that have cautioned me against imagining that I have a special right to suffer or a special right to think I know how the world should be or a special right to tell others how to live or a special right to announce how God is speaking to another person. So, I have resisted the idea that my suffering is any worse than anyone else's suffering.

But, in the last five years, I have had to revise my opinion about my suffering.

About six to eight years ago, a therapist told me that borderline personality disorder may soon be renamed to be *Relational Disruption Disorder*. Or, rather, she told me that there was discussion about renaming borderline personality disorder. Wikipedia now lists a second name for borderline personality disorder which is "EUPD" ("emotionally unstable personality disorder"). In case you're wondering why the word *borderline* appears in *borderline personality disorder*, I will tell you: the "border" part of "borderline" personality disorder comes from the border between psychosis and neurosis. When borderline personality disorder was being identified, around 1940, it seemed to researchers that patients were on the border between psychosis and neurosis.

I have thought a lot about relational disruption as I have learned more about how I came to have this horrible problem in my life. I know a lot about what happened to me. I also was in many, many sessions of the first module of Marsha Linehan's DBT program. In the first module, she provides patients with an explanation of borderline personality disorder and how one comes to have borderline personality disorder. Marsha Linehan is a very smart person, and she speaks very carefully. She does not suggest in this presentation that she is giving an exhaustive explanation of borderline personality disorder and its causes. Indeed, no one knows all about its causes.

I know three things about the cause of my difficulties:

1. I was born with a body that happens to experience acute physical, mental, and emotional responses to all kinds of stimulation. My brain and my nervous system take in information from my environment and from my insides that some people's brains and nervous systems don't notice. I can't turn it off. I am aware of things that other people might not have to be aware

of. This is not good or bad. It is simply the way I was born. Some people are born this way; some people are not.

2. I was born into a family in which there was no adult capable of nurturing a child.

3. I was very sick at a very young age with a life-threatening illness.

Research has told us that there is a genetic component that predisposes some people to borderline personality disorder. I cannot comment on whether I have any genetic predisposition.

We also know from research that it is almost universally the case that persons who suffer from borderline personality disorder in adulthood were born with the kinds of brains and nervous systems I am describing in myself. That is, they were born with bodies that were turned up on high volume for input from sights, smells, sounds, and feelings on their skin coming in from the environment around them. Not only that, they were born with bodies that were turned up on high volume for sensations coming from inside of them.

Hyper-sensitive to the world and to themselves.

Think about that for a moment! A newborn is breathing for the first time. She has never breathed before. I am 60 years old right now; I have breathed a lot. I am accustomed to breathing. Right now, it doesn't feel strange or frightening. But on the day I was born, born with a body that is especially sensitive to stimulation of all kinds, I began to breathe, and my brain was flooded with sensations I did not understand and had never felt before. It probably freaked me out. Where some other infant born without this acute sensitivity to inner sensations would begin to breathe and experience it as unusual, I may very well have experienced it as disturbing and frightening and upsetting. Or not. We have no way to know.

Quite a bit of research has been done, as I said, that tells us that adults who suffer as I suffer are adults who have bodies with brains and nervous systems similar to mine.

Here is the important part of that discovery: researchers suspect that children who receive that much input from the environment and from inside their bodies do just fine if they have one or more adults in their life who are capable of successfully nurturing them in a manner that gently leads them to be able to grow to adulthood in a way that they can be friends with their body. If there is a calm adult in their life who can be friends with her own body (or his own body) and comfort this child when sensations bother the little one, then this tiny creature learns from being around a person who understands being friends with her own body how it can be to be calm and be friends with one's own body.

This requires the presence of a primary caretaker who is, at least to a great extent, a completely grown-up adult human being. It means that the primary caretaker needs to have a lot of her own childhood issues resolved. It means that the primary caretaker needs to be comfortable with her own body and needs to be able to calm herself when she is upset. It means that she needs to be in control of herself when she is extremely happy. In other words, she has to be ready to be a competent parent.

Tiny infants born with these very sensitive bodies and born to people who are not really ready to be parents do quite poorly in the world. If they are born to parents who are wildly unable to be parents, such as my parents, they do extremely poorly in the world.

Thus, point number two: I was born into a family where both my mother and my father did not have nurturing skills. There were some things they were able to do. They were very competent at changing diapers and feeding children. Unlike my mother's family of origin, we did not go without food. Additionally, we were never smelly because we were not bathed or because we were wearing poopy diapers.

Although we had pajamas with holes in them because we were so poor, we had well-mended clothing when we went out the door. We were not beaten. The three daughters of the family did receive care that was adequate in the areas that one can observe with the eyes and nose. One would have to use one's ears and one's understanding to comprehend the emotional abuse.

Finally, I was born with especially light-colored Norwegian and Irish skin, strawberry-blond hair and skin that does not produce very much oil. (This coloring tends to be coincident with dry skin.) In fact, my skin produces so little oil that it breaks open because it is so dry. When I was an infant, my skin would break open and become infected with the everyday staph and strep germs that are around us all the time.

Sometime between my first and second birthdays, I developed sepsis. The way the story was told to me by Suzy, my parents were informed that I would not live. Penicillin did not solve the problem.

Suzy told the story this way, "The phone rang. Bill answered and it was a doctor from New York State. Bill talked to the doctor, who told him that there was a new antibiotic that was approved in the United States but not in Canada. Bill talked to the doctor but did not tell me what the conversation was about. Without consulting me, he told the doctor that we would use the antibiotic for Jansen."

Obviously, the new antibiotic, which was a penicillin-related drug, was effective, and I am still alive! But when I was a one-year-old, I weighed 20 pounds and when I was a two-year-old, I weighed 21 pounds, so I'm sure I was not thriving.

This kind of childhood illness is a trauma that leads to problems in adult life.

I have taken quite a detour from my intended topic: I have, for a long time, resisted the idea that my suffering is somehow special. But in the last five years, I have had to reevaluate my suffering in comparison to other human beings.

Let me comment on my suffering as a newborn and as an infant.

When I think about how much my skin hurts every day right now, I realize that my skin must have hurt a tremendous amount as a newborn and as an infant. The skincare routine that limits the pain I have these days involves four kinds of ointment and two kinds of cream. It requires a daily shower and a special kind of clothing. It requires a certain kind of washing machine. It requires living in a home that's free of perfumes and scented products. It requires having no pets and having no upholstered furniture. There is an entire dust mite routine involved.

For those of you who have similar sensitivities, you will know that I am leaving out 100 other details. I am certain that infant Jansen was not covered head-to-toe in medicated ointment every day, so I am sure the pain was excruciating.

Let me say, as I have said before, that I am not implying any intention on the part of my parents to allow me to be in pain. They would not have known that I was in pain from my skin. Even knowing, they would not have known what to do.

I did not learn how to care for my skin until I was hospitalized with an infection on a large part of my skin on the first day of 1985. If you know the painful infection called "impetigo," imagine having that on 30% of your skin.

I was admitted to the hospital at the University of Minnesota on January 1st that year. It is a teaching hospital, of course, and one of the students, having been sent to take a complete medical history as an exercise, asked me if I knew why I had been admitted. Naturally, I thought I had been admitted because I was suffering from a skin infection.

The student informed me that I had been admitted mostly because, in the United States, a person with skin infected like mine was something the teaching dermatologist would not normally get to show students. I didn't care. I was happy for the steroid ointment that was being applied five times per day.

The professor who was the medical doctor teaching dermatology there at the University of Minnesota sent me back to my city to the local teaching university hospital to a professor, also a medical doctor, who researches atopic dermatitis (eczema) and who was happy to have me as a person with a skin to study. That professor taught me how to take care of my skin, and I have been more comfortable since then. But I am still in pain from my skin each day.

Bill once commented on baby Jansen saying, "I remember carrying you up and down the hall, and you would cry and cry. Nothing I could do would get you to stop crying."

His two sentences are open to various interpretations. From my knowledge of Bill, I don't think he was expressing any compassion for baby Jansen. He was telling me how distressing it was for **Bill** that baby Jansen would not stop crying. I would like to believe that he was not saying that he was angry and annoyed with baby Jansen. However, I have to say that I did experience him as being angry and annoyed with my son when my son behaved in a manner that inconvenienced Bill.

I've read a bit about what happens to infants in a family that has no nurturing adult and also has yelling and screaming fights between the parents and knives flying through the air. Even when the yelling and screaming were not happening, Suzy and Bill were angry.

Born so sensitive, I was, undoubtedly, aware of the hostile atmosphere that existed all the time. In addition, Suzy was not capable of being happy that I was a new little human being in the world. Suzy did not know that her children were going to be actual human beings and require her to set aside what she needed for herself in order to meet the needs of her children. She would have been horrified to know this; she was quite resentful of the energy and time she had to spend on her children.

As an infant and small child, I would have perceived it. Think about this: I was a baby and small child, and when I cried out for food or something I needed, the person who arrived was the provider of the necessities but was also angry and resentful — resentful of me.

This is where a child suffers from relational disruption. The part of the brain for human connection that should be developing in the first year of life gets confused. If the primary caretaker is also angry and hostile, even unconsciously angry and hostile, even angry and hostile though she does not wish to be, the bond between mother and child is strange and warped.

Because Suzy was my first contact with humanity, the damage that was done will simply never be undone. My relationship to human beings was disrupted by that twisted and misshapen initial relationship. The damage is so severe that there is a part of my brain — a structure in my brain — that is not correct because of the combination in my mother as caregiver and antagonist.

I have one comment to make before I answer the question, "Is my suffering worse than the suffering of most human beings?"

The comment that I wish to make is this: what follows logically from the discussion above is a discussion of the evidence that the damage done to my brain is somehow far-reaching and permanent. Or, rather, what follows logically is a discussion of the veracity of my claim that my relationship to human beings was so deeply affected by Suzy that the damage cannot be undone. That will have to wait for a subsequent chapter.

So, how bad is the pain of borderline personality disorder? The question is difficult to answer. Pain is difficult to quantify. Both emotional pain and physical pain are difficult to quantify.

Occasionally, someone will suggest to me that I am not "entitled" to be in pain because I have had enough food to eat every day of my life and I have a house to live in. The implication is that the people who are dying of starvation are the people who really are entitled to say they are suffering.

However, there is reason to believe that people living in parts of the world where the resources for survival are quite limited are not especially suffering emotional pain. That is, even in parts of the world where it is very difficult to get water every day, for example, communities still have an abundance of human love and connection. Communities that have a lack of food do not suffer from extreme unhappiness. Places where there are not enough apartments, such as Hong Kong, are not places where human happiness goes away.

There seems to be no evidence that having the necessities of life means you are exempt from suffering and no evidence that lacking the necessities of life causes emotional suffering.

Because I don't have access to my emotions, I can only report thoughts. I know I have emotions, so let me report how I feel with a few thoughts:

- I feel I have to earn the right to be alive every day by doing a sufficient number of useful tasks;
- I feel no one is ever going to help me with anything;
- I feel I am not a real person;
- I feel it is crucial to hide who I am because I am unacceptable;
- I feel I am a fountain of mistakes.

It hurts a lot.

Recently I have decided that yes, my suffering is significantly worse than the suffering of most persons who are not mentally ill.

I observe that people who are more normal than I am (whatever that means) might feel that they have made a mistake, but later they feel okay again.

I observe that people who are more normal than I am (whatever that means) might feel disconnected and lonely, but later they feel okay again.

I observe that people who are more normal than I am (whatever that means) might feel useless, but later they feel okay again.

I feel like I am a mistake, and I am disconnected from humanity, and I am of no use all day, every day.

I have been in therapy for 45 years working on this.

It hurts a lot.

If alcohol made me feel better, I'm sure I would be a drinker.

If gambling made me feel better, I'm sure I would have figured out how to be a gambler.

Indeed, if any impulsive behavior provided relief, I would be doing it!

If you have any ideas on what would provide relief for me, let me know!

Bungee jumping? Cocaine? (I don't know how to get cocaine.)

I have no trouble understanding why someone would gamble away a life's savings in an afternoon.

For an afternoon free of this pain I would do almost anything.

Well, I guess I wouldn't hit a human being.

The pain is terrible. There is no other way to say it.

It hurts a lot.

CHAPTER 11
Suicidality, Self-Mutilation

Recurrent suicidal behavior, gestures, or threats, or self-mutilating behavior. (DSM-IV)

TRIGGER WARNING: IF you have problems with suicidal ideation, suicidal behaviors, or self-harm behaviors that can be triggered by reading about the suicidal ideation and self-harm of others, you will want to skip this chapter.

Perhaps the very worst words to speak to a person who is suffering terrible emotional pain are these: "God never gives us more than we can handle."

Obviously, this is not true. People kill themselves. People can feel so much pain for such a long time that they simply cannot handle any more. People choose to die. It is simply not the case that no human being is burdened by more challenges than they can handle.

I do not believe that God is the source of our problems, in any case. I am a liberal Christian, and I do not believe that God has a plan for my life; I believe that life unfolds in ways that are mostly unpredictable. I believe that God is powerful, but I don't believe that God has the power to inflict cancer upon somebody or cure somebody else of cancer. Cancer is not under God's control. As much as I would love to write, here, about God's power, that is beyond my scope. And there are fine theologians writing about God's power — God's great power — in an area called "Process Theology," that do it better than I can.

In many ways, I believe I am on a path to a suicide death. Until quite recently, I had a belief that suicide was not an option for me. I believed this because I have a son. It was my belief for 30 years that, having brought a child into the world, I was committed to staying alive. However, I recently have changed.

I spent decades in an endeavor which I believed to be the work of building a family. I was mistaken. Now I am divorced, and my son chooses not to have any contact with me. I was not aware that both my son and my husband suffered from disabilities that made compassion and kindness especially challenging for them. I was slow to understand that they had different goals for their lives than I have for mine.

I was my son's first contact with humanity; in some way, I represent for him what it is to be human. I think it would be damaging to him if I were to die of suicide. I believe it would not be good for him to be the son of a mother who died of suicide. Still, he has made the decision not to be part of my life, and my suffering is extremely intense. If he and I have no relationship, there is a limit to the amount of suffering I'm willing to endure to protect him.

I do not see a great deal of hope for my suffering to be reduced anytime soon. After 45 years of therapy, I am not expecting psychotherapy to provide a reduction in my suffering. I cannot form happy relationships with human beings. So, I do not expect any people to come into my life who will somehow magically make my daily existence more pleasant.

When I read research about borderline personality disorder, I see that some successful treatments can lead to patients having fewer impulsive behaviors that make their lives worse and can lead to patients going to the emergency department less often. But I have not seen any research that measures a reduction in suffering or an increase in life satisfaction. I am already fairly free of impulsive behaviors that make my life worse, and I rarely go to the emergency department.

The culture I live in perpetuates the story that we can be happy all the time. There is no workable model for suffering is part of a normal day. I have been part of a church for many, many years, so I know many people well enough to talk to them. But I find that people are uncomfortable hearing me say that I am suffering. Sometimes people want to fix me. Often people want me to stop talking about suffering — it makes them uncomfortable. And there are very few who are willing to hear the truth that my suffering is my overwhelming experience every single day.

Recently I had emergency surgery for the removal of my appendix. After my surgery people brought me food and called to see how I was doing. Three weeks later I was in the hospital for seven days being treated for suicidal ideation. When I got home from the psychiatric hospital, no one brought me food or called to see how I was doing. The stigma of mental illness is still very strong.

Suicidal ideation frightens people.

I have a very good thinking mind. When I look at my situation using my reason and using logic, I cannot see how things might get better. I am already medicated quite well. I have had all the available psychiatric treatment. The damage to my brain cannot be reversed. The suffering is likely to continue at this level indefinitely.

Suicidal behavior by people with borderline personality disorder comes in many varieties. There are successful suicides and there are suicide attempts. It is unclear the extent to which a person is really wanting to die when they exhibit suicidal behavior. It is unclear how much they actually wanted to die when they actually do die, and it is unclear how much they actually wanted to die when they do not die.

I believe that any person who attempted suicide was a person who was in a great deal of pain. Talking to a person who tried to kill themselves, I always proceed with the knowledge that a suicide attempt is a method of communication. It screams, "Something is wrong! Something is wrong! Listen to me! Listen to me!"

I feel suicidal every day. Every day, I wish I did not have to be alive. But I am not a person who will ever have a suicide attempt (in contrast to a successful suicide event). I am extremely competent. If I ever actually want to die, I will decide to die and 20 minutes later, I will be dead. I am extremely competent. I will not fail.

A few years ago, at Christmastime, my psychiatrist was concerned that I would kill myself and persuaded me to be hospitalized. I made an appointment at a local psychiatric hospital for an intake interview on December 23rd. Unfortunately, I am so high-functioning that I, apparently, didn't know how to act crazy enough to be admitted to the hospital. Even with a letter from my psychiatrist explaining my needs and asking them to hospitalize me, they would not admit me!

Borderline personality disorder is so terribly painful that sufferers try to express their pain in many ways. Suicidal gestures are common. I seem to be free of suicidal gestures and threats. I guess that's good.

I have not escaped the self-mutilation troubles that so often accompany borderline personality disorder.

I was not aware until I was about 55 years old that I engaged in self-harm. At that time, I saw a new psychiatrist at my HMO, a psychiatrist who asked me better intake questions. I had been asked the same series of intake questions by many psychiatrists in many settings by the time I was 55 years old. The standard set of intake questions includes, "Do you hurt yourself or cause yourself pain? Do you cut yourself with razor blades or burn yourself with cigarettes? Do you have other behaviors you engage in that cause yourself pain?"

I had always answered "no" to those questions because I did not cut myself with razor blades or burn myself with cigarettes. Until this new psychiatrist questioned me, no one had asked me any follow-up questions that were subtle enough to elicit from me the relevant information. She asked me if there was anything I did that caused me pain which was in some way helpful to me.

I said to her, "Well, I was helping to set up tables at church yesterday and one of the tables pinched me and caused this wound." Here I indicated a small break in my skin where the table had cut me just a little bit. I continued, "I remember thinking that this was good because it would hurt the rest of the day."

I explained to her that I always kept some sore on my body open so that it hurt, because the pain was helpful to me. I added that I was surprised to hear her ask that question, because I didn't know that having a painful sore on my skin to help me through the day was something a psychiatrist would know about.

I was 55 years old, and I had been seeing therapists for 40 years. 40 years! And no one had explained to me that self-harm is motivated by an attempt to take care of oneself. I had not known that I was engaging in self-harm because no one had asked enough questions or educated me about self-harm.

This book is the story of my mental illness. Foolish therapists and psychiatrists have failed to recognize my illnesses because I cope so well. Not thinking to educate me about common psychiatric problems, they miss an opportunity to find out from me that I'm suffering from common psychiatric problems. In fact, it has often been through my own research that I have discovered my difficulties. This also is a clue to the reason that so many very troubled people go into the professions of therapy and psychiatry themselves. No one is really helping them, and they are attracted to fields of study where they can actually learn something about their own difficulties. (And don't get me started on why very spiritually troubled people end up in seminaries.)

To get back to self-harm, the self-harm I inflict daily on my skin is not enough even to require a Band-Aid. Well, I say that "on a daily basis," but there have been times when it has been a little worse than that.

You may recall that I said that I would scratch myself until I bled when I was a little, tiny child. I suspect that I did not get attention from my parents unless I was literally bleeding. So, the connection between pain and blood and getting some of my needs met, even a little, probably goes back a long way. Also, because I am in a state of dissociation all the time, I don't really feel pain. I don't really feel anything.

In this regard, my self-harm is different than that of some other people. Often a therapist will ask me how I was feeling before I harmed myself and what the effect was on my state of being. That is, each therapist I work with wants to help me figure out what function the self-harm has in my life. But I do not have access to any inner states. So, I am not aware that there is any particular inner state that exists before I harmed myself or that, after harming myself, I feel any different.

My best understanding of my self-harm is that it is a method of communicating to myself that my suffering really is very terrible. I cope so well that, absent the self-harm, my life could look like everything is fine for weeks and months and years at a time. My best guess is that the self-harm is functioning to remind me daily that I am coping extraordinarily well but that things are not fine, are not fine, are not fine, are not fine. Otherwise, I think I would go crazy!

My life looks like I am doing okay. But I am **not** doing okay.

I was in treatment at a very fine DBT clinic for more than two years. The goal of that treatment was to arrest the self-harm cycle. In two years, my therapist and I could not find any motivation for me to stop the self-harm. I simply do not wish to stop. I understand that a person who is normal (whatever that means) does not cut into herself with a tool. I understand that a person who is normal (whatever that means) wants to stop cutting herself. I was willing to entertain the idea of developing some motivation to stop cutting. But we could not find any motivation for me. Avoidance of pain was not a motivation because I do not feel pain. Finding a substitute for the function of the cutting was unsuccessful because the cutting is playing a role that is important for me. We just could not find anything that would make me wish to stop.

One psychiatrist I had at the HMO told me that he could not ethically do this, but, if he could, he would recommend cutting to me. He would do so because it was minimally dangerous, and it was working for me. When he thought about all of my challenges and the many things I could be doing to cope, he thought my very small amount of self-harm was probably an excellent choice. Then he would quickly add that he could not actually say that to me because it would not be ethical for him to do so. (Then we would chuckle together.)

Often, I think about the idea that some people who have been abused turn their anger outward and hurt others, while some people who have been abused turn their anger inward and hurt themselves. I believe this is true. Usually, this division occurs simply according to who has been conditioned, culturally, to be an oppressor and who has been conditioned, culturally, to be oppressed; that is, who is male and who is female.

However, with borderline personality disorder, the sufferer of either gender or any gender identity has already been conditioned to believe they are unimportant and of no value. This is the reason that suicidal ideation and self-harm prevail even though they are turning-inward and attacking-the-self behaviors. The primary caregiver did not validate and nurture the little person so that he or she or they would know they are valuable as a self. In adulthood, they act out this learned lack-of-value in horrible ways.

One more thing: do not imagine that you can fix things by simply saying to someone who feels that they don't have value: "You are important. You are valuable." The sad truth is that words do not reach this kind of pain. The abuse that caused borderline personality disorder was inflicted at a young age and was inflicted with more than just words. It did not simply create bad neurological pathways in the brain; it damaged the structure of the brain. There is substantial evidence that talk therapy does not solve these problems.

People mean well; I understand that people mean well. People mean to be kind when they tell me that I am important and I am valuable. However, people say things to me that fall upon my ears in a way that is received by me as unkind. Can you see that it is almost like walking up to an insulin-dependent diabetic and saying, "I wish upon you a better-working pancreas. May you have a pancreas that works better"?

Nothing you say to a person whose pancreas stopped working when they were eight years old is going to cause the pancreas to once again begin to make insulin. We do not walk up to people whose pancreas does not make insulin and say to them words that we imagine will somehow help. We know that we have no words that will help.

Yet, for some reason, people imagine that they are going to soothe my mental illness or even cure my mental illness by speaking words to me. So poor is their understanding of mental illness that they imagine they have some power to affect it! What amazing hubris!

If mental illness were cured with words or thoughts, I would not be ill. I am very good with words and thoughts. I am very, very smart. I am articulate. I have an extraordinary vocabulary, and I can put together sophisticated sentences. Indeed, when speaking to people in the general public, I often have to modify my sentences before I speak them because many people cannot understand a sentence that begins with a dependent clause! (I kid you not.) Yet I am profoundly mentally ill, and I suffered terribly.

Words and thoughts are of no use against borderline personality disorder.

I am not saying that one should not educate herself about her illness. Of course, it is useful to know what kinds of challenges she is facing. I study the latest research, and I also study the different kinds of treatments to glean what I can from each approach. I also learn about the world's enduring religions because spiritual growth and personal growth and recovery from mental illness are all part of the same process of human growth. So, I am not saying that words and thoughts are to be dismissed or ignored. But they do not solve the problems of mental illness or take away mental illness.

If you are one of the mentally ill, I sympathize with you, for I am sure you have to endure people trying to cure you with words.

If you are wanting to be kind and caring to folks who suffer from mental illness, do not say, "You are valuable." Instead say, "I am so sorry that you suffer from pain, that terrible pain of feeling not valuable. I wish you could feel that you are valuable. I wish I could magically give to you the feeling of being valuable. If I could magically give it to you, I would do it."

CHAPTER 12

Emotional Instability

Affective instability due to a marked reactivity of mood (e.g., intense episodic dysphoria, irritability, or anxiety usually lasting a few hours and only rarely more than a few days). (DSM-IV)

HAVE YOU EVER known someone who has mood swings? Most of us have known a person who has fluctuations in mood, usually a noticeable change from being in a good mood to being in a bad mood all of a sudden. That person usually also goes from being in a bad mood to being in a good mood all of a sudden.

Mood swings are normal in everyone from time to time. There are people for whom mood swings are normal, day in and day out—that's just the way they are. They are not mentally ill. They are simply people who have an emotional temperament that happens to make them move quickly from one kind of emotional inner experience to another. But the instability of mood that is seen in many people who are suffering from borderline personality disorder is like mood swings times one hundred: not a gentle ride on the playground baby swing, more like a mood bungee jump.

Let me tell you about one of the outcomes of mood bungee jumping. Most people who are afflicted with borderline personality disorder at the level of intensity that I am afflicted find it difficult or impossible to behave in a manner that allows them to have stable housing.

Some decades ago, quite a lot of these people may have been institutionalized in our state hospitals. Was that a good thing? On the positive side, they were probably warm and probably had food (though not always). On the negative side, oversight was minimal, and abuse was widespread. One thing is certain: persons who cannot behave in a manner that allows them to have stable housing are a conundrum for us as a society now. They live in cars or sleep outdoors. Sometimes they have housing for brief periods or long periods and are, then, once again in a housing crisis.

There is a connection between having a mental illness that causes one to have intense changes in one's mood and being unable to have stable housing. If, without your consent, your body and mind suddenly go into an intensely angry state without any event triggering that change, or, perhaps, when some event that does not make other people angry occurs, people around you are unlikely to think, "I'll bet this person has some kind of horrible mental illness. I'll bet she has no control over what happens to her body and mind. Probably she needs our compassion and kindness right now. Let's not call the police. Let's ask her if she needs any food or a cup of coffee. Let's ask her if she needs a place to wash her clothes and take a shower. If we demonstrate that we care about her and want her to have everything she needs in life, she'll probably calm down and feel much better."

No, people are terrified, as well they might be. A mentally ill person whose body and mind have thrown them into a mood bungee jump of anger can act violently. We should be worried about our safety in such a situation. It is necessary to call for law enforcement officers. Compassion is not going to keep us from getting hurt.

These kinds of behaviors prevent some people suffering from borderline personality disorder, at the level of profound affliction that I suffer, from being able to be good enough neighbors in a home or apartment or hotel room. Even when they experience an emotional bungee jump of friendliness, their friendliness might be super-duper over-the-top friendliness. The accompanying behavior may be intrusive, loud, inappropriately self-revealing, and too persistent. What is being experienced by the mentally ill person as an outpouring of love-of-neighbor can be experienced by the person in the apartment next door as some kind of creepy stalking behavior.

Why, then, you might wonder, am I still alive at age 60? Why have I not succumbed to the illnesses and injuries of a person who has slept outdoors consistently? How have I managed to live for 40 years of adult life in suburban homes which I have owned?

Let me disabuse you of the notion that it is because I am wealthy. Many a wealthy mentally ill person is homeless. It does not make any difference that a person has financial resources if the police come in response to a complaint that you are so angry as to be a danger to your neighbors or so friendly as to be a danger to your neighbors. Even though being wealthy can get you out of some problems, even problems with the police, officers will take you away if you are a danger, no matter how much money you have.

No, I did not start out with any extra money that made it possible for me to hide out in suburbia. However, I did start out in a deep state of emotional freeze.

I had no idea that I was living a life that was emotionally frozen during the years that I was walking through the motions of getting married, raising a child, earning a master's degree, homeschooling my son, teaching as an adjunct professor, and participating in the life of my church. I'll give you an example of my frozen life: I recall going to the zoo with my boy when he was about 2½ years old. There was a pen with a split-rail fence inside of which was a group of miniature goats. Some children were allowed to go in, a few children at a time, to be with the goats under the supervision of a zoo employee. My little son was an extremely cautious child. He had no interest in going into the pen of goats, but he was very interested in watching the other children touch the goats.

My very cautious son did not even want to be close to the split-rail fence. Indeed, he did not even want to be standing on his own feet. He was a little bit afraid. So, he and I were standing about 6 feet away from the split-rail fence, and I was holding him. I am a teacher in my soul. I cannot help teaching — I teach everyone all the time. I probably annoy people a great deal by teaching them whatever pops into my mind whenever I am near them. It was for this reason (and because I was a good mommy) that I was saying to him, "Look at those goats! I see some goats butting their heads together. They bump their heads together like that because they are playing. It's kind of funny, isn't it?"

I used the word *butting* and in the following sentence said they bumped their heads together for him to be exposed to new vocabulary. What I know now about the tone of voice that I employed is this: I used an amused tone of voice and gave a little chuckle because I had learned to imitate the emotional expressions that were appropriate to the situation in which I found myself. At the time, I would have told you that the tone of voice I employed could be explained by my genuine amusement at the behavior of the little goats.

I want you to understand the contrast. At the time, I thought I was amused. Now, I know I was imitating amusement. Looking back in my memory, I can see that I was imitating normal life, without knowing it, from my very earliest memories up until that very fine therapist helped me discover that I do not have access to my emotions.

This is how I was able to stay in my suburban home. I had very good behavior. I had good behavior because the intense emotional reactivity of borderline personality disorder is not available to me.

I have been assured by every therapist I have ever seen that I have emotions. I believe it. I certainly have thoughts in my mind that are clues to the emotions I must be having. For example, after ending my relationship with the man that I married, there were two Christmas seasons during which I did not have anyone to buy a gift for, and I did not receive any gifts from anyone. Presumably, that made me sad and distressed. When the thought went through my mind, "I have no one to buy a gift for and no one is giving me any gifts," I would begin to weep. However, I do not know what it is to be sad. I have never felt any sensation that I would describe as sadness. I think it would be a mistake to say that every time tears come out of my eyes, I am sad. Probably that is not true. I am only guessing that I am sad. All I know is that I would start to cry.

To make any progress toward getting well, I will have to, first, be able to be genuinely mentally ill. That is, there is no way to go from a state of being profoundly frozen to being somehow more completely human and more completely whole without passing through the state of being the mentally ill person that I am.

I am convinced that there are intense episodes of anxiety and sadness and euphoria present in my life. I am convinced that they are not the normal changes of mood that people who do not have borderline personality disorder experience. I am convinced that I do not have access to them. I am convinced that this does not mean that they are not interfering with my life. I am convinced that I will need to experience them in some genuine way before I can learn to manage them.

So, in a way, I will have to get worse before I can get better.

There is some good news in this area. It happened that my son graduated from college in 2010. At that time, there was a recession around the world, and there were no jobs for young college graduates or anyone. My son lived in my home, with me and my husband, for a longer period than I had anticipated he would. In many ways, this was a blessing.

My husband, a software engineer and an Aspie (a person on the autism spectrum who has the kind of autism that was once diagnosed as Asperger's Syndrome) makes a lot of money. Thus, it was not a burden to have my son in the household, and we were not suffering because of the global downturn of the economy. But, from time to time, I would speak to my son about the amount of money he was spending. I had not anticipated giving him an allowance for years and years. Still, I had not anticipated the global economy suffering a downturn just when he was launching himself into adulthood.

On the occasion of one of these talks about money, my son said to me, "Why is it that you always talk to *me* about money? Why are these conversations about money never conversations with you and me and Dad?"

"We've tried that once in a while," I answered. "You may not have noticed, but, when we do that, Dad speaks three sentences about money and the fourth sentence is about death. Money, money, money, death."

My conversation with my son about money and Dad and death segued into a conversation about the terrible anxiety that his father was suffering. At that time, my husband, now-former husband, was a person who would not have agreed to go talk to a counselor. So, my son and I decided to tell him that we three needed family therapy. We cooked up the idea that the family needed therapy to talk about money (which was not really untrue).

I want to say how proud I am of my son for caring so much about his father and wanting to help his father who was suffering so much from anxiety. And I want to give credit to my former husband who showed up for every counseling session even when the counselor was telling him that he needed to make changes.

My son and I basically sat quietly while the counselor worked with the very anxious breadwinner of the family. Eventually, the economy picked up; my son got a job and an apartment and found an awesome sweetheart; my son moved on from the family counseling; the sessions became marriage counseling.

Here's my point: my son didn't need me anymore, or rather, didn't need me as a mom for everyday things. My son has been diagnosed, also, with autism spectrum disorder. There is a lot to say about autism spectrum disorder, but I will say just a little about my specific situation. It is clear to me that my son was born with a brain that is, in some ways, like his father's brain and like his grandmother's brain and like his great-grandmother's brain. It was not difficult for me to figure out that my son needed some special kinds of teaching. I am a teacher in my soul. I sent him to first grade full-time at the public school to see what they could do for him.

The public school was not able to educate him adequately. As an example, I'll tell you that they did not have in the first-grade classroom a book for him to read that was at his higher reading level. The classroom teacher did not consider this a problem. "He can read the picture books," she said.

It was the school librarian who was looking out for the gifted children. She made sure that my son had appropriate reading material, but that meant he had books available to read at home, not appropriate books to find on the shelf as the other children had.

Also, I could see that the social atmosphere of public school would provide my child with a milieu of messages that he was not normal (whatever that means). The public school would have been a negative influence in his life.

He did go to the public school for several hours every day during the years I was homeschooling him. We pursued a kind of education called "unschooling". There were many interesting unschooling activities and groups in the area and we enjoyed the company of people who share the outlook that children, like plants growing from the ground, are going to grow into the people they are meant to be. Parents do not get to choose what kind of person their child will be.

My son happened to be a child who was okay spending most of his day with me and other adults, and we had a neighborhood populated with several families whom we really liked. It was my privilege to spend so much time with him and give him many, many lessons per day (as many as happened by in teachable moments) in the area of understanding human beings and interacting with the world in socially appropriate ways.

Like many people on the autism spectrum, my son experienced human development in a manner that was a little different than what is typical for most persons growing from infancy to adulthood. Intellectually, he was quite sophisticated at a young age. When he was six, he said to me in the car one day, "Mom, you and Dad put out the presents and say that it was Santa Claus, right?"

I replied, "I don't think you want me to answer that question."

He said, "I think you and Dad put out the presents." Again, I told him that I didn't think he wanted me to answer the question, and I added that I thought he would feel sad if I answered the question. He was only six years old, but he could think abstractly already. Already he could deduce from my comment, the comment that I thought he would feel sad, the conclusion that it was, in fact, the case that his parents helped Santa Claus. I knew that he could make this deduction, and I was hoping that the conversation could end with my comment that I thought he would feel sad.

The little six-year-old boy insisted that he wanted me to answer the question. "Yes," I reluctantly said, "the adults do put out the gifts that you see from Santa Claus."

Then tears appeared (not mine). Oh, my goodness!

"Sweetie, let's pretend I didn't say that." Now I had a chance to play the role of the mother who knows her child so well that she knows he is both intellectually sophisticated and also still a little boy. "Let's pretend we can roll back time a couple of minutes. We're going to pretend we can roll back time and you didn't ask me that question and I didn't answer it. Okay?"

So, I led him through a little mind game, as we drove down the road, and we pretended we could roll back time. Together we pretended he had never asked the question and I had never answered it. His ability to believe in magic was still intact. While he was intellectually very advanced for age 6, he was exactly age-appropriate for age 6 in his ability to believe in magic. Thank goodness! That was a tool we had in our toolbox that day.

As is typical for many people on the spectrum, my son's development in the area of social interactions proceeded more slowly than is usually seen in those who are neurotypical. There were times when he would call me from the college campus in Vermont needing some coaching or support around interactions with human beings. It is often the case that young people who are ready to go across the country for college are also ready to handle interactions with peers without help from their mother. Or, maybe I should say, it is often the case that young people do not want help from their mother when they are 18 or 19 or 20 years old. My son was still asking for an occasional bit of advice. I tried to tread lightly, remembering that he was a full-grown adult person even if he was asking questions that someone else might have asked at a younger age.

The symmetry is worth pointing out: at a very young age, he was asking very sophisticated intellectual questions; at a somewhat advanced age, he was asking social questions. Neither of these is good nor bad. I have a very strong conviction that one should raise the child that she has. This young male person was entrusted to me to nurture into adulthood. It was my privilege to do what I could to help him to become the person he was meant to be. He was going to do that at his own pace regardless of anything I did or did not do. It was my job to raise the child I actually had — not to force upon him some timetable devised by me or someone else.

So, you can see that it was not a problem for me that I was still doing some work each day as a mother until the economy picked up, and my son was able to get a very good job and an apartment. He had his own social group. I found myself no longer putting daily energy into any tasks of parenting when I reached 55 years old.

It was at that point that I began to emerge from my frozen state. It was a blessing that that young man had been in my home, because I found myself in marriage counseling. I had learned that I did not experience different inner states. I had more time and energy to attend to my own needs. One further extremely significant event occurred at the same time: Suzy, the primary abuser from my childhood, died. Things began to change.

I have begun to emerge from the frozen state. The only positive result is that it is a step on the road to becoming more fully human. My behavior is much less socially acceptable. I am no longer able to maintain relationships with human beings. I have lost my marriage and my sisters. However, all of this is necessary because the only way that I was able to remain in a marriage that was harming me was by being in a deeply frozen state. And the only way I could interact with my sisters was by allowing behaviors that were harming me.

It is a horrible thing for me, a person who has had good behavior, to see myself behaving in a manner that I wish I did not. For example, one day at church, the greeter at the door said, "Wasn't that potluck dinner last night fun?!"

When I was in my frozen state, I would not have had any reaction to this question, and I would have answered in a socially acceptable manner saying, "Yes, I really liked the casserole you brought."

Now, no longer being able to be socially acceptable, I am triggered by being confronted with a question that has only one socially acceptable answer. I feel compassion for this greeter at the door. She does not mean to be offensive. Nevertheless, she is offending me. She has greeted me with a question that has only one socially acceptable answer. One is required to say yes. It is simply not okay at a suburban Christian church to be greeted with the question, "Wasn't that potluck dinner last night fun?" and answer, "No, I am severely mentally ill, and I do not experience pleasure. Nothing is ever fun for me. I attended because it is important for me to go through the motions of a normal life. I am offended by your question. If you are going to be a greeter for our church, please say something to people that is welcoming. Use an open-ended question. Do not say something manipulative — something that forces them into just one answer."

The above response, which is not okay at my suburban church, is the response I gave. It upset the unfortunate recipient of my diatribe enough that the pastor heard about it. I was held responsible, by the pastor, for speaking in a manner that was not acceptable to the woman at the door. It is simply not the case that I will be able to educate an entire congregation to understand that some people are severely mentally ill, and we should be sensitive to them.

If I could arrange it, everyone in the congregation, this greeter included, would modify their behavior to avoid asking questions as if all people experience pleasure. Already we have learned not to ask questions as if all people are married to an opposite-sex spouse. There is the potential to learn. I think it will happen — but I am 50 years before my time.

In closing, let me say that it is likely that any success in establishing a connection with my body that allows me to access physical sensations will bring with it even more troublesome behavior. I would not say good things are on the horizon. However, I have no choice but to continue to try to access physical sensations. Staying in a state in which I cannot access anything about my body is not an acceptable plan.

There is no plan for me other than trying to get well. What would be the other option? To consciously choose to remain in a state of illness is not something I will do. I will not sit around being ill. I will work to get well. I will move on toward human wholeness. That is what I do. I will move on.

I will work hard.

I will grow.

I will try.

CHAPTER 13

Emptiness

Chronic feelings of emptiness. (DSM-IV)

EARLIER IN THIS narrative, I related the story of discovering that I do not have different inner states. That is, I am numb inside all of the time. For me, that is just the way it feels to be me.

I don't know if the DSM's emptiness is the same as my numbness. I suspect that chronic feelings of emptiness are feelings that nothing really matters — life has no meaning. I have heard people describe the feeling that their body is empty or numb as a feeling that is connected to having lost any reason for being alive, having lost the motivation for doing daily activities. I have heard people talk about doing something routine, such as brushing their teeth, and they are thinking, *Why am I brushing my teeth? What sense does this make?*

If feelings of emptiness seem chronic, they persist over a long time or they are constantly recurring. But we do not describe something as "chronic" if it has no starting point and has never been interrupted. It is just there, like existing. This was the difficulty for me when I was trying to understand that I do not have differing inner states. It was almost by chance that I found out that I was numb inside without having had some experience of being not-numb-inside as a contrast.

So, it makes sense to ask, "Is it also the case that I have lived all 60 years of my life feeling that nothing I do has any meaning? Have I lived plagued by a cloud of thoughts and impressions that there is no reason to be alive?"

Well, I know some answers to some parts of those kinds of questions.

About 10 years ago, I began to understand that I do not believe that I am real. I had been in cognitive therapy for 35 years by that time. I had become very good at noticing a problematic behavior and asking myself what kind of thinking was behind it. I was delving into some issue that was pressing in my life, asking myself what kind of thinking was making me behave in this not-very-productive manner, when I discovered that the behavior was predicated on a belief that I am not real; that is, a belief that I am not an actual existing human person.

Being quite startled by this discovery, I began to explore it in my mind — *in what way am I not real?* I wondered. I came up with the answer that I don't have hands and feet. I certainly do purchase socks when I need them. I also own shoes. So, is it not an irrational belief that I don't have hands and feet? No, I simply don't identify with the hands and feet that are attached to this thing that people call "Jansen." I don't have any sense that those four things, two hands and two feet, are mine.

I continued to think about this, off and on, for the ensuing ten years. If I had a dissociative disorder, then I would have episodes of losing the sense that I am connected to my body. However, my sense of connection or disconnection to my body does not change. It is exactly the same all the time: I have no experiences that lead me to believe that I have hands or feet or knees or a nose or…anything.

Sometimes I describe it this way: I believe that Barack Obama is a person and that he is alive right now and is doing something somewhere. I believe that Jansen Vee is a person and that she is alive right now and is doing something somewhere. I have no idea why people think I am Jansen Vee and not Barack Obama. I feel no more connection to Jansen Vee than I feel to Barack Obama. I have an equal sense of belief in each of those two persons, and I have had just as much experience that confirms the existence of Barack as I have had experience that confirms the existence of Jansen.

Here's another way I describe it: I have learned about China. I believe there are people in China. I believe there are people in my state. I don't know why people think I am in my state and not in China. I have not had any experience that would lead me to believe that I am in my state and not in China because nothing that has happened to me here in my state has happened to anyone real. There is no Jansen that I know of. (I once spent 36 horrible hours in an emergency department in their "psychiatric boarding model" when they would not hospitalize me. The cruel social worker, upon hearing me say that I did not know why people think I am in my state rather than in China sneered, "Then why don't you move to China?")

Does this feeling that I am not real put me in the DSM category of borderline sufferers who experience chronic feelings of emptiness? No, I don't think so.

The feeling I have that I am not real is continuous, not a feeling that comes and goes. I wouldn't use the word *chronic* to describe it. And I don't have any doubts about the meaning of life or the significance of everyday tasks that are connected to the sense of not being an actual existing real person, so I don't think it is like the usual emptiness.

The source of my inability to feel real is clear. My primary caregiver in infancy and childhood was my mother, Suzy. Suzy was a profoundly narcissistic and very damaged person. She knew that she wanted and needed things, but she did not know that any other entity in the world wanted and needed things. Everything else in the world was a tool that was, at any given time, either doing or not doing what she wanted it to do. Some of those tools walked and talked.

Suzy did not know that I was real.

It has become known in popular culture, now, that parents can help their children by providing a language for the little ones' feelings. Many parents now know that there is an advantage to choosing to say to their child, "You are feeling sad and angry that we have to put these nice toys away and say goodbye to Grandma and leave." This use of language to help children process what is happening to them and have a vocabulary for their inner experience is part of mirroring — a parent's accurate reflection of a child's expressed thoughts and feelings.

Suzy was unable to be an adequate parent in the area of mirroring. She could not accurately reflect my expressed thoughts and feelings because she had been damaged so badly herself that she did not know that I had thoughts and feelings. A person who is damaged to the point of narcissism believes that her thoughts are occurring in the mind of her child. She believes that her child feels the way she wants her child to feel.

Suzy is no longer living, but I can tell you it was excruciating to be around her. She suffered horribly. She was full of unpleasant energy, always trying desperately to get things right so that she could show that she was an acceptable person. She had to be the most beautiful person in the room and the richest. She had to be the thinnest and have the most expensive clothes. She was not able to give a gift without telling the recipient what a very special gift it was from a very special art gallery on the Coast. It was so painful to witness!

Suzy had no idea that she was suffering, and she was not open to any discussion of anything spiritual or therapy-related. She had used every bit of her very substantial courage to survive and get an education and raise three daughters and move into the middle class. She had not one ounce of courage left to tackle her personal, deep pain. If she had ever begun to know what she had done to her children, it would have killed her.

Nevertheless, she did not know that I wanted and needed things. When she gave birth to children, she knew she would need to change diapers and put meals on the table, but she didn't realize that her children would need her time and her money. Every time I was forced to go to her to ask for something (and I tried never to do that), she was startled. She never adjusted to the fact that her children would need $15 for the gymnastics uniform or need a signature on a permission slip. She was surprised every time. She simply did not understand that this little tool was demanding her attention. It was as if the washing machine had acquired a voice and was asking for $15.

As a result, Suzy did not do mirroring. She did not say, "Oh, yes, it hurts when your knee is skinned like that. And it's even worse when you're hungry. You haven't eaten since breakfast. Let's clean that up and bandage it. Then we'll get you a snack and you'll feel better." Those words and the actions of caring for a child's wound and feeding the child would provide a nurturing bridge that would connect her to her painfully wounded body and allow her to understand that people can be part of the answer when we are in pain.

What I learned was that people can make the pain worse. They don't notice that I'm bleeding, and if it is called to their attention, they express concern for the furniture – concern that my blood should not stain the furniture. I learned that human beings did not know I have pain, so I did not have pain. My body was a source of problems for the big people whom I had better not annoy, as they are the source of my food and shelter.

I learned no one is going to help me when I am in pain. When I have pain, I should hide and be sure I don't cause problems for anyone. This was consistently the message from both parents, not because they meant to send that message, but because they were so damaged themselves.

I have had very painful skin from the day I was born. I almost died from a skin infection in my second year of life. As an infant, I cried and cried and cried — probably from my skin's pain. Unlike my sisters, I am a person who picks up so much information from my surroundings that it overwhelms me. I can't shut it out. So, it's likely that I figured out within a month or two that the adults became distressed when I cried.

Children naturally deduce that they are the cause of family problems. They do. And, in this case, I would have correctly figured out that my crying made the adults uneasy and unhappy. Thus, it may be the case that I began to suppress my crying even when I was just a few months old.

This would have been the beginning of my mental illness — I probably began to take action to keep my parents happy even before I could form complete thoughts about what was going on. I likely slid into the role of being the identified problem and acting as though I was quite powerful, powerful enough to keep the family happy or make the family unhappy, even before I could walk and talk. This is a scenario that occurs in troubled families. It leads to mental illness in certain kinds of babies born into certain kinds of families.

It isn't anyone's fault. It's the coming-together of several unfortunate circumstances.

Before I could walk, I was exhibiting self-harm. I would scratch myself until I bled. The pictures of little Jansen at 8- and 9-months-old show her with socks over her hands to keep her from scratching herself. How sad! This, too, may be a clue that patterns of undesirable behavior were not understood as warnings that something was amiss. I speculate that I had trained myself not to use crying to get needed care, so I learned to use dripping blood to get needed care. This may be what was happening.

Because Suzy could not understand that I experienced pain, I did not express pain with words or sounds. I was in my 50s before I reached back in my mind to assess childhood events with questions about pain.

In 1985, when I was 25 years old, I was hospitalized with a skin infection and subsequently received intensive instruction concerning caring for my skin at the teaching hospital from a specialist researching atopic dermatitis. For the first time ever, I learned how to take care of my skin so that I am mostly comfortable every day.

Looking back at my childhood, I remember Suzy washing my entire skin with pHisoHex (hexachlorophene detergent skin cleanser). pHisoHex carries a warning, now, about systemic toxicity relating to the central nervous system. I want to state once again that Suzy had no intention to poison me or cause me pain. However, in retrospect, I can imagine it was a horribly painful experience to be washed that way.

Sometimes people ask me, "What did your mother do when you told her that she was hurting you?" or "What would your mother say if you told her it was strange that she was always surprised that you needed money for something?"

These questions are nonsense! I grew up in the kind of family in which it would not have crossed my mind to tell my mother she was hurting me. I did not know my mother was hurting me. I did not know I was experiencing pain. If you raise a child in an environment in which no adult is aware that this child can have pain; if you raise a child in such a way that you never noticed the child is in pain and acknowledge it — never acknowledge pain — never — the child will not know that she experiences pain. I could not tell my mother I was in pain because I did not know that pain was a thing!

Emerging into adulthood from a family that seemed, on the surface, to be an ordinary family but was, actually, profoundly broken, I was at a terrible disadvantage. Children who are beaten know that they have been beaten. A child whose parent burns her with cigarettes does not doubt that she was burned with cigarettes. A boy or girl who is sexually abused does not have any doubt about being raped or sexually abused (well, some sexual abuse is weird and subtle).

But when I started my life as an adult, there was no one in my life, other than my two sisters, who believed that anything bad had happened to me. In fact, a great many people believed I had had two wonderful parents. People went out of their way to tell me how wonderful my parents were. When I graduated from high school at age 17 years and five months, I did not know that I did not feel pain; I did not know that I did not feel real; I did not know that my parents were both narcissists. I did not know that normal parents *want* to talk to their children. I did not know that normal parents *want* to feed their children. I had no idea about the details of the bizarre family I had come from.

Nevertheless, I had begun at age 15 to tell trusted people that I was being raised by a homicidal mother. By that, I meant that I could sense that my mother, on some level, did not want me to exist. I was beginning to understand that anything I did that made me a human being, different from her, was deeply disturbing to her. I could not yet articulate this, but I could grasp on a non-intellectual level that she could not tolerate anything I did that differentiated Jansen from Suzy — Jansen could not like different food than Suzy; Jansen could not like a different dress than Suzy; Jansen could not like a different book than Suzy; Suzy was so profoundly narcissistic that she did not know that Jansen was not Suzy.

Suzy was a homicidal mother in the sense that she reacted with extreme distress any time any daughter did anything that made that daughter a human person. The only daughter she wanted was a daughter who was an extension of Suzy (and reflected well upon Suzy). This was not because Suzy intended to be cruel or unkind or malicious. She herself was damaged.

Yet, Suzy was, in fact, cruel. She was, in fact, unkind. She was, in fact, malicious. But she was none of those things because she wished to be. She had been, herself, horribly damaged. And I'm not sure she really did everything she could to recover.

But how would I know?

CHAPTER 14

Anger

Inappropriate, intense anger or difficulty controlling anger (e.g., frequent displays of temper, constant anger, recurrent physical fights). (DSM-IV)

SUZY WAS ANGRY all the time, which makes me wonder if she should have been diagnosed with borderline personality disorder herself. I wonder if I am angry all the time. I wonder if I have inappropriate, intense anger or difficulty controlling anger.

Happily, I do not display a problem with recurrent physical fights! Physical fights are, I suspect, seen in male patients or seen in patients who identify strongly with the characteristics attributed to males in our culture more than patients like me, comfortably identifying as female. I have not struck a human being, and also, I do not throw objects or smash things.

When I was 18 years old, I spent the summer as a counselor at a Girl Scout camp in the Pacific Northwest. In the middle of the night, one night, my partner counselor and I confronted two girls who were eating bread and peanut butter from the stash in the unit cupboard. I hope you will infer that the girls were not supposed to be up and help-ing themselves to a snack in the middle of the night.

I was standing close enough to one of the girls that when she gestured broadly with her left hand, I found myself reaching out with my right hand to catch her hand in mine. I was horrified. I had never before touched a human being when I was in the midst of a conflict with him or her. I was shocked at what I had done. I was appalled. I was over-come with distress at my action.

I decided on the spot that I would never touch a person if I was arguing with them ever again. Was this a reaction to the violence in my family of origin? It's an interesting question because I have only two memories of actually seeing violence as a child. However, I have no confidence in the absence of other memories as any type of conclusive evidence that I did not witness a significant amount of violence.

As an example of my lack of confidence in my assertion that I saw only two acts of violence, the incident of the knife flying across the room in Canada, my first memory of life, I do not count as violence. That type of interaction occurred regularly in my family. The two incidents of violence I am willing to admit are those in which someone actually struck another person in my presence. The case in which Bill pointed to a wound on his face and said to Suzy, "And who did *this*?!" I call a reference to violence, not an instance of my witnessing violence.

When I grabbed at the hand of that Girl Scout, I was not yet aware that I was numb inside. I couldn't have articulated the disconnect between observing that we were in conflict and the absence of any physical sen-sations that I have been told others have when they are angry. But I knew I didn't want to aggress physically on others in that way.

So, I will take credit for being aware of anger in myself at a fairly young age. I will take credit for being able to decide before I was 20 years old about how I would manage my manifestations of anger, at least a decision about extremes in my behavior toward human beings concerning my own anger.

I feel it is setting the bar very low to decide not to touch someone when I deduce that I feel anger toward them; thus, I feel I am taking credit for a decision that earns me not too many stars in my crown.

Yes, I would guess that I am angry all the time. A great deal of my anger might come under the category of righteous indignation. I notice thoughts and behaviors that indicate intense anger that arises quickly when someone mistreats a vulnerable person. At the same time that I am plagued by this righteous indignation that I cannot turn off, I have terribly poor boundaries. It is common for people struggling with borderline personality disorder to have poor or no boundaries in relationships with other human beings. This makes anger especially difficult in relationships.

When I feel righteous indignation — anger about something's being not the way it should be — my inability to understand boundaries between myself and another person causes me this kind of difficulty: I think that if I simply tell the other person what they are doing wrong, they will understand me and fix the problem. This makes perfect sense to me. Maybe you can imagine why this makes perfect sense to me. I have very little access to my emotions; I compensate by watching my thoughts and behaviors; I live my life by analyzing what I am doing and what I am thinking; after analyzing what I am doing and what I am thinking, I make decisions based on that input. Of course! If I just inform the other person, with careful analysis, of the exact and precise behavior that they are doing incorrectly, they will be grateful for their newfound knowledge and they will change!

When *I* gain newfound knowledge about something I am doing incorrectly, I change, don't I? Of course, I do! I am perfect!

Well, the above is a little peek into the way that my mind works. It is the sad truth that black-and-white thinking creeps in. Black-and-white thinking, actually, does not creep, the way a hermit crab or a snail might creep. Black-and-white thinking strides in like an attorney who can't imagine that anyone would expect him to wait his turn to speak since, after all, he is an attorney! But wait. No, that's not it. Black-and-white thinking rushes in like the out-of-breath messenger you are not supposed to kill.

Let me give you an example. I was at church on a Sunday morning. After the first hymn and a prayer, the children were invited to come forward and sit with the Minister of Youth and Families for the children's talk. The minister said, "Have you ever had a time when you had a disagreement with a friend or someone you were playing with? Or have you ever been talking to someone that lives where you live, and the talk wasn't very much fun, or people weren't having a happy talk?"

She waited for the children to think about this, and some of the children volunteered answers to her questions. As usual, some of the words that were given in response addressed her topic and some of them were more random. She did her usual very good job of affirming the children whether or not their comments flowed into her theme.

After a while she went on, "You know that yucky, uncomfortable feeling in your belly when you feel angry with someone in your family or someone you really care about? When we're mad at somebody that we love, it doesn't feel good. We wish that feeling would go away."

It was at this point that I had two or three thoughts about that and noticed a desire to stand up and interrupt the children's talk in a loud voice. I knew, from this evidence, that I was angry. Can you guess what type of righteous indignation I was experiencing? Can you?

The minister did not ask the children what their experience was when they were angry with someone they cared about. She did not ask them what it was like for them to be mad at someone they loved. She informed them that it felt yucky and uncomfortable, thus establishing in their young minds that it is normative to feel bad if you are angry at someone in your family.

This minister is someone whose situation I know fairly well. She has two children still living at home and a loving spouse. She is wonderfully suited to be a mother. She is devoted to the task of meeting the needs of her children. She did not remember, statistically speaking, we know that this collection of children is just as likely to include children who are being beaten or sexually abused or starved or emotionally abused or burned with cigarettes as any other group of children in the United States or in the world. The fact that all of these children are clean and are wearing cute little outfits means nothing, statistically, about the likelihood that they are living in homes where they are being harmed by their parents.

To suggest that anger toward their parents is something that ought to make them feel bad is a horrible message to communicate in a Christian church (or anywhere). Anger is a gift from God. In a fully-grown-up human being who does not have any significant mental health problems, anger is an indication that someone has trespassed upon our legitimate territory — physical territory, emotional territory, personality territory, decision-making territory, some kind of territory.

A child may indeed become quite angry if Mommy will not let him have seven cookies instead of eating a healthy dinner. The child's mind has not matured to the point where he can understand that eating seven cookies instead of having some healthy food is unwise. An adult may have to make that decision for him. The adult is trespassing on his decision-making, but it is appropriate to do so under the circumstances. But that same child may be angry if Mommy harms him in some manner that we, in this society at this time, identify as child abuse.

I am not sure I can support the minister's suggestion to the child that he should feel bad about being angry with Mommy about the seven cookies. It is entirely age-appropriate to be angry with Mommy about the seven cookies if you are five years old. And, if you are suffering child abuse, it is entirely appropriate to be angry with Mommy without feeling any bad feelings about holding that anger or even actively keeping that anger alive if you are five or 15 (or 25 or 35 or 45 or 55).

It is righteous indignation over this kind of issue that sweeps over me. I become fierce. I want nothing more than to speak to that minister and tell her she is harming small children right in front of my eyes by teaching them that the anger they feel toward that abusive parent is something that ought to be experienced as negative. I am fierce and furious, and she is going to feel my wrath!

Now, shall we discuss if that is inappropriate anger? It is certainly intense anger. I can tell you I did not stand up and interrupt the worship service. Shall we discuss if, when I did speak to her, that was a display of temper? Shall we discuss if I had difficulty controlling my anger?

All of those are possible discussions. But here are some others: shall we discuss whether I am especially insightful? Shall we discuss whether I am especially courageous in confronting authority? Shall we discuss whether I am a powerful advocate for the voiceless? Shall we discuss whether I am ahead of my time? Shall we discuss whether I can see things others miss? Shall we discuss whether the terrible abuse that I suffered has given me almost nothing except deep compassion?

Yes, I am angry pretty much all the time. The world is doing terrible things to small children. The world is doing terrible things to the elderly. The world is doing terrible things to those who do not have a great deal of money. The world is doing terrible things to many human beings.

I don't watch television, because I cannot tolerate knowing what is happening in the world. I do not expose myself to any news source at all. At the time of this writing, candidates are seeking the nomination so that they can run for president of the United States in the election that will take place in the fall of 2020. I don't know who these candidates are. I know that the president right now is Donald Trump. I have seen photographs of him, but I have never seen him on any kind of video, and I have never heard his voice. I have never read any words that he has spoken. I have never read any quotation of his words.

My PTSD is triggered so easily, and I get so upset by the mistreatment of human beings, that I have to quarantine myself from all news of what's happening in the world. I simply cannot tolerate the realities of our world. However, I think about the books written by Laura Ingalls Wilder such as *Little House on the Prairie*. A few hundred years ago, some people lived in their home and did their daily tasks without input from the outside world week after week and month after month. I am not isolated in the manner that little Laura Ingalls and her family were, since I have a church community and other contacts. But being connected to all of the news of the whole world is, by no means, the way people have always lived.

I have a long way to go in managing my anger because it does alienate me from many people. It alienates me from people who are insensitive and unkind. It alienates me from people who are selfish and greedy. It alienates me from people who are harming others out of indifference or for pleasure. It limits me to associating with people who are kind and caring and sensitive and sweet and nice. Oh, my goodness! What a loss. (Not.)

CHAPTER 15

Transient Paranoia

Transient, stress-related paranoid ideation or severe dissociative symptoms. (DSM-IV)

SOMETIMES I WISH I could be paranoid like other people with borderline personality disorder.

It's very common for sufferers of borderline personality disorder to believe intensely that people in the world are against them. They can have a persistent and deep belief that everybody is, for some unknown reason, unkind to them in a manner that people are not unkind to other human beings. They will find evidence for this at every turn.

When something happens to me that is not to my advantage, my illness causes me to glance around swiftly to see who is at fault. Because of my illness — because of my brain — because of the damage that was done to my brain — I will immediately look around to see which human being has purposely inflicted this insult upon me.

Oh, how I wish I were not intelligent and could not analyze my experiences in the moment! I think it must be easier to live with this illness if one is permitted the simple approach of accusing whoever happens to be nearby or happens to be involved and erupting in anger toward them. Unhappily, I actually do this often enough to get myself in trouble with people. But more often, I can see myself having the experience of a person with borderline personality disorder. Then I feel obligated to do something other than accusing the nearest human being.

Perhaps the worst part is that my brain is wired, not for human connection, but for this other thing: my brain is wired to believe that people are trying to hurt me. As I walk around in the world, every person I see is identified by my damaged brain as someone who is planning to do something bad to me. I have to work against that reality all of the time.

There is a story from my childhood that I recall vividly. It illustrates to me the extent to which I perceived human beings to be impediments in my world, the extent to which I perceived human beings to be huge problems for little Jansen when I was only nine or ten years old.

I recall sitting in the family station wagon, parked on a side street near a lake in the city. When I say we were parked on a side street, I mean that we were parked on a street that was not the street that goes around the lake. The reason we were in that neighborhood was that we had come to a musical instrument shop because my older sister's violin needed to be repaired. Not being interested in going into the shop, I was sitting in the car (probably reading a book) and noticed a full-sized concert harp displayed in the shop window. I was imagining that it would be interesting to strum the strings on the harp. Then I was fantasizing about the circumstances under which I could be permitted to do that.

In my young mind, the only circumstances under which I could imagine being allowed to do something I wanted to do, that is strum the harp strings, were if all the human beings on Earth, except me, were to disappear. Let me say that again: my fantasy was that all of the human beings on Earth would need to disappear, except me, and I would be able to walk into the shop and walk up to the harp and see what it was like to strum the strings. In the reality of that nine- or ten-year-old girl, there was no other way that she would ever get to do something she wanted to do.

I saw every human being as someone who was trying to keep me from doing the things I wanted to do. My imagination could not stretch far enough to think that anybody would help me by taking action that would enable me to do something pleasurable or interesting. It would never have occurred to me to look to my parents to advocate for me to do something I wanted to do. It would never have occurred to me to ask the shopkeeper. In my world, everyone was trying to keep me from doing things that I wanted to do. That was simply the obvious reality.

This story, together with my ability to write this book, really causes me to ask myself, "What happened to me?" This illness is not especially unusual. What is quite unusual is that I know that I have this illness. It is quite unusual that I can reflect upon this story from my childhood and identify it as an instance of a fairly young person already manifesting a horribly damaged mind.

I do **not** look back at the story and say to myself, "Look, even at a young age, I understood that human beings were evil and were trying to hurt me. Look, how wise was I to know at such a young age, that I needed to protect myself from a world of evil humans!" No, I do not look back at the story and draw that conclusion.

What happened to me? It is exceedingly strange.

It would not be strange if I had grown as a human person or grown in my faith to the point where I understood that people do not mean to hurt me. I know some people pursue spiritual practices who come to the point where they know that the hurts they receive from other people are usually unintended. They come to be such big people themselves that they can set aside quite a bit of the pain of interacting with other people. That happens fairly often. I have heard about that. I have met people who have been able to do that.

But I have not achieved any particular heights of spiritual growth. What I am describing is entirely different. I have become aware that my brain is not right. I can watch myself identifying every human being as someone who is going to harm me. I am aware that my first reaction to difficulties in life is a burst of strange energy focused on finding the culprit amongst the people nearby. I can tell that this is an illness. I can watch myself acting out a brain problem. I have a thinking mind, and I have a broken brain. They seem to be able to function simultaneously.

I guess it would be easier if my thinking mind were able to believe the messages of my broken brain. I think that other people suffering from borderline personality disorder at the level of severity of my suffering probably are not able to do anything other than believe the messages of their strangely wired brains. Have you ever tried to convince someone whose mental illness causes them to have thinking problems that the world is different than they believe? You will not succeed.

To say this succinctly: I almost wish I were paranoid.

The second section of this part of the DSM-IV traits of borderline personality disorder talks about dissociation. I have learned, by searching the Internet, that it is almost universally the case that dissociation is discussed as something that happens in episodes.

The typical question from a psychiatrist concerning dissociation is whether I feel like I'm sometimes experiencing life separate from myself — as if I were watching myself on TV. Long ago, when I first began to be interviewed by psychiatrists, I answered no to those questions, of course. I would still answer no if I were asked a question about watching myself on TV today.

But I did try to explain my concern about having strange experiences to someone when I was just 18 years old and a college student at an East Coast university. Much to the credit of the student health system there, they did have me evaluated by a psychiatrist for a possible dissociative disorder.

The best I could do to describe my reasons for being concerned about myself was this: I don't know why people think I am in this body. For example, when I am sitting in the waiting room and two people are talking to each other and then the two people get up and they walk out of the room as they are still conversing, I think it is very strange that, as they walk away, I can no longer hear them. I don't understand why they can be talking to each other — and I know they are still talking to each other down the hall — but I can no longer hear and follow the conversation. I was completely immersed in the conversation while they were in the room with me. Why am I now not in the conversation? I don't understand why I am here and they are now somewhere else.

The psychiatrist did a very good and thorough evaluation. I still don't know what kind of dissociation I have, if it is dissociation at all. I suspect it is some kind of experience that has some kind of name. Someone reading this book will know more than I do. I'm sure that there is no group of unintegrated pieces of the personality of Jansen inside of me, as is sometimes the case for people with borderline personality disorder. In my case, I have a strong suspicion there is no personality in there at all. I suspect that my experience is related to the absence of any core sense of knowing who I am. I am confused that I am not Jane or John or Joan because I have no way to know that I am Jansen.

My biggest impression, here at the end of commenting on these aspects of borderline personality disorder, is that I am profoundly ill. By that, I do not mean to say anything bad about myself. Some people are tall. Some people are born with dark hair. I was born into a family that damaged my brain and now I am profoundly ill. It is simply a fact.

This damaged brain is something that I have to deal with, just as I have to deal with my skin which needs medication every day. People who are afflicted with this kind of damage to their brain at this level often do not do as well as I do, if we use survival to age 60 as a measure of success. I am not certain that these 40 years of adult life that have been quite miserable are any kind of measure of success.

Please keep in mind that I have no training in the area of evaluating myself or anyone for borderline personality disorder. My comments are all based on my own experience, my reading, things therapists have said to me, things psychiatrists have said to me, and, undoubtedly, ideas I have picked up from our culture. I would not be at all surprised if, perhaps, 20% of the ideas I have presented as factual turn out to be not quite true. These comments are my ideas, meant only to be the thoughts of someone who is a sufferer.

And finally, again, let me caution you against thinking that any book, any one book, or even any two or three or five or ten books that you read could allow you to diagnose yourself or anyone else with a mental illness. Persons who are professionals in this area are trained with much more than just academic ideas. They are also trained by other human beings who have experience dealing with real human beings. Consulting a respected professional would always be my advice.

So, yes, sometimes I wish I could be paranoid like other people with borderline personality disorder. Instead, I am burdened with knowing this paranoia is not the case, no matter how much it seems to be true.

CHAPTER 16

Jansen's Peculiar Gifts

IT HAPPENS THAT I was born with a brain that remembers words set to music very easily. I memorize songs, especially hymns, without even trying.

One of my favorite hymns begins, "Jesus shall reign where'er the sun doth its successive journeys run." My favorite stanza of this hymn is:

> *Let every creature rise and bring*
> *Peculiar honors to our King,*
> *Angels descend with songs again,*
> *And Earth repeat the sweet Amen!*

This use of the word *peculiar* does not mean that every creature should bring strange or odd honors to God. *Peculiar* has several meanings. *Peculiar* can mean strange or odd, as it does when we say, "She wasn't looking her best that day; she was wearing a peculiar hat." Sometimes *peculiar* does not carry any negative connotation but only means "uncommon," as when we say, "She is a quilter, but her husband has the peculiar hobby of stuffing and mounting bats." In this hymn, however, the word is used to mean belonging characteristically or exclusively to some person or group or thing. So, the peculiar honors, here, are the praises and songs characteristic of the individual creature that is bringing them to God.

In the 1980s, I was studying in a Lutheran seminary, planning to be a Lutheran minister. I did not follow through with that plan, having felt a strong anti-calling to the ministry at the time that they asked each of us in my class to go and buy a robe. (When I say I felt an "anti-calling," I am making a little inside joke. In certain kinds of Christian social circles, one does not say she decided to become a pastor, one says she was called to be a pastor by the Holy Spirit. I was uncalled to be a pastor when I could not envision myself wearing a robe – an alb, actually – and shaking hands with parishioners after a worship service.)

Anyway, while I was still a seminary student, it fell to me to plan one of the daily chapel services that took place on campus. The parameters of the service were fairly well established, but I did get to choose the hymns. One of the hymns I chose was this one which begins, "Jesus shall reign." I built the prayers for the chapel service around the hymn's text.

I received a favorable critique of my work from my supervising professor, and his only suggestion was that it may have been more appropriate to build the prayers around the reading from the *Bible* rather than the text of the hymn. I'm not sure — I think a lot of Christians who attend churches that use hymns absorb a great deal of theology from the hymns they sing.

Because my father was the pastor of a Lutheran church at the time I was born and until I was five years old, I learned a lot of hymns very early. When I was five years old, Suzy announced that she was moving to the United States and Bill could come with her or not, as he chose. He did leave the ministry and moved to the U.S. with the family.

I was the only family member of the five of us – that is, Suzy, Bill, my older sister, me, and my younger sister – who consistently attended church after the move to the United States. When I was eight years old, a friend at school told me about the children's choir at the church that our families both attended, and she explained exactly how I could show up and be included. It was within walking distance, so I just went there. I participated in the children's choirs at the church until Suzy moved us away when I was 15.

During that time, I memorized many, many hymns. My point is this: the use of the word "peculiar" to mean "characteristic of a certain person" came to me through the hymn and was, as far as I knew, the standard use of the word. Thus, it comes naturally to me to say that I have peculiar gifts that have helped me survive borderline personality disorder.

Yes, I have strengths that have allowed me to survive borderline personality disorder. Quite a few of them are the strengths that you would expect to find in somebody who has not succumbed to this illness. But I also have some **peculiar** gifts that have helped me survive borderline personality disorder.

I have a pervasive pattern, in a variety of contexts, of the following:

- I talk despair, but I act hope.
- I persist.
- I am an excellent problem-solver.
- I have an unusual ability to observe my own behavior.
- I have an exceptional ability to analyze all kinds of things.

The more obvious skills and abilities which keep me going require very little elucidation. I will list some of them here:

- I always take my medicine as prescribed.
- I always go to all of my appointments.
- I do everything I am told to do that might make me better, such as meditation, exercise, trying to eat well, yoga, trying to sleep well, trying to be on a schedule, not isolating myself, learning self-help skills, practicing self-help skills, journaling, calling the helpline, doing assigned reading, keeping records, going to classes, reading research, and other things I can't think of right now.
- I remain in a mental state of openness toward help from providers whom I trust. My criterion for trustworthiness is this: I trust persons with training in Western medicine, and I trust persons with training in other forms of treatment of human difficulties that have a long and established history. For example, acupuncture is not Western medicine, but it has a long and established history. Massage is not Western medicine, but it has a long and established history. I stay away from things that are new and trendy. I stay away from practitioners who do not have training from some reputable institution or apprenticeship program.
- I do these four things listed above regardless of feelings of hopelessness and despair.

My peculiar gifts and abilities that have resulted in my survival to the age of 60 are worthy of further comment, as the subjects of the following chapters.

CHAPTER 17
I Talk Despair, but I Act Hope

I GENUINELY EXPERIENCE despair; I genuinely experience hope — at the same time.

I have a good thinking mind; I have a very good thinking mind.

There is an upside to this and a downside to this for me as a mentally ill person. The upside is that I can understand the tasks and challenges in front of me and bring to them an organized, triaged effort. Also, I can discuss my needs using the vocabulary that the professionals who are helping me are using. However, the downside is that I have a larger grasp of the width and depth of my difficulties than most mentally ill persons.

When I talk about my particular mental illness, I talk despair. I don't especially mean to do this — it's just that the facts, as I understand them, are pretty bleak.

I was slow to come to believe the facts.

The first time that "borderline personality disorder" was put on my medical chart as one of my diagnoses, it may have been there quite a while before I knew about it. I discovered its presence on my chart when I first could examine my diagnoses by logging into an account with my HMO. Having discovered that my psychiatric diagnoses included depression and some other things and borderline personality disorder, I asked my psychiatrist at that time to remove it from the list. He did so.

I was too distressed about the diagnosis even to ask the psychiatrist what borderline personality disorder was and why it would have been connected to me. Rather than taking the opportunity to learn something about the struggles I faced, I ran away from the information.

But later, another psychiatrist felt it was an appropriate diagnosis and, rather than simply putting it on my chart, she told me she was considering putting it on my chart. I must've made a frightened face or an appalled face, because she immediately said that she felt I would be only mildly borderline and that borderline personality disorder, like all human things, fell on a spectrum. I was at the less severe end. (I believe, now, that I am not, actually, just mildly afflicted, but that I present so well that I appear to be less severely afflicted than I am.)

When I was in treatment for my-not-very-bloody daily cutting problem at the DBT clinic, my therapist, after getting to know me, said, "Considering what you are facing, it's amazing that you don't live under a bridge." This comment had a deep impact on me. When she said this, I began to consider seriously that I should embrace borderline personality disorder as a reality for myself.

This same therapist and I, more than once, got out the DSM-IV and read through the criteria for diagnosing borderline personality disorder to see if I seemed to have five or more of the listed characteristics. Each time she helped me understand that I did meet the official diagnostic definition for borderline personality disorder. She helped me understand the difference between using that reality as information and misusing that as any kind of label that would cause me to limit, in my own mind, possibilities for my life.

Although it was frightening to understand the extent of the damage that I had suffered, it was also, in a way, a source of hope. Many of us have known the unsettling feeling of being aware that something is not quite right in our bodies or in our lives and having no idea what the problem is. A diagnosis may not change anything about our situation in the short term, but there is a small amount of relief that comes from knowing more about what is happening to us.

As I have learned more and more about what has happened to me and what is happening to me, my talk has become more and more despair-talk. Knowledge about the lack of success in the treatment of borderline personality disorder, in contrast to the treatment of depression, for example, is discouraging. Encountering quite a few professionals who have never before seen a patient who is alive at my age and has my kinds of challenges has added to my knowledge of the severity of my affliction. That is distressing. Having never met another patient who has the same kinds of challenges makes me feel weird and isolated. Despair results from all of these.

I have been known to say that there is no hope for me. "I am just going to suffer, intensely, like this, every day until I die," I say this with some frequency.

The strange thing is that my behavior does not reflect this belief at all. Every day I have two or three new ideas for things I can do that might lead me to some kind of better life. My imagination and my creative mind just keep coming up with ideas and thoughts and plans for new and different ways to manage my life so that things could be better. Novelty bursts forth from my creative brain unimpeded by my despairing thoughts.

Let me give you some examples.

Here are some of the things I have thought of in the last week which I have not implemented, and I may never implement, but I think they would help me:

- Meditate on Suzy's being enticed into a heavenly party by God's angels. The party would be very attractive to Suzy and would be taking place behind very large, heavy doors. If, in my meditation, she could be persuaded to go into the party and the doors could swing shut, she would not be able to bother me here on Earth anymore.
- Make a playlist of the music mentioned by the woman who spoke at the Wednesday night Lenten service.
- Make a PowerPoint presentation of pending issues that my therapist and I have discussed and left unattended.
- Attend the dance class given by the woman who preached at church. She teaches a dance class aimed at encouraging people who have never danced before.
- Make a more attractive outfit to wear to the gym so that I won't be so embarrassed about being so fat.
- Write about what I learned from talking to the young man whose mental illness was a little bit like mine but who was noticeably worse than I am.
- Write about what I learned from observing the woman at the therapy group whose mental illness was a little bit like mine but who was noticeably worse than I am.
- Consider whether I know things that other people don't know.
- Think about writing an essay or book about overcoming hypervigilance.
- Consider whether I am beginning to feel hunger.
- Think about why I was ashamed after I spoke my name at the Centering Prayer gathering when the leader introduced me in a way I didn't like.
- Make a list of things I need from a therapist.

- Make a list of things a therapist should never say to me and a list of things a therapist could say to me that would always be helpful.
- Make some alternative to cheddar cheese using cashews and nutritional yeast but mostly cheddar cheese.
- Think about something as a reward to give myself or to do at bedtime as an alternative to eating a large bowl of ice cream.
- Consider cutting myself more at bedtime instead of eating ice cream (probably a bad choice).
- Make a white dress for Easter.
- Think about ways to exercise without having to get down on the floor which triggers my asthma if the floor is dusty.
- Consider whether my task at this time in life might be to take care of this person named Jansen whom I don't like that much.

My mind works like this all the time. I am always thinking of some new things to try.

Not only that, when something goes badly, I move on and try something else. I don't seem to have the ability to give up. I talk despair, but you would not guess that I have any despairing thoughts from watching my behavior.

I truly do not know what this is about. I feel angry — or rather, I am guessing I feel angry — when somebody is cheerful about my behavior and tries to tell me that I am a very positive person. I do not experience anger as a physical sensation, but I always want to tell them not to say those words to me.

For example, one pastor at a church I attended was fond of finishing up any conversation we had by pointing out to me what a good job I had done of taking care of myself. Maybe this was just her standard phrase for ending a conversation. It struck my ears as entirely too upbeat, especially because we had always been talking about some story of mine of suffering and struggle.

I would point out to her that I did not perceive that I had done a good job of taking care of myself. She did not seem to recognize that there was a pattern to our interaction, or at least, she did not modify her conversation-ending style. Finally, one day I said, "You can be as cheerful as you wish, but it does not mean that I am not severely mentally ill and in a lot of pain!"

I am guessing I was feeling invalidated. Invalidation is a big issue for people with borderline personality disorder. Invalidation is the technical term for the experience of interacting with someone and having them say or do something that leaves one feeling as if she doesn't have the right to be the person she is. Borderline personality disorder is induced in children by massive invalidation over long periods coming from their primary caregiver. Thus, invalidation causes a strong reaction throughout their life.

I refuse all cheerfulness! I refuse to be happy! I refuse to be positive! I am determined to be miserable!

Well, those statements are not precisely true. I simply react strongly when someone is unable to tolerate the reality of my pain and, to relieve their discomfort, informs me that I am doing just fine.

The truth is that in many ways I am doing just fine. The other truth is that in many ways I am not doing well at all. These are both true at the same time.

I genuinely experience despair; I genuinely experience hope — at the same time.

It's confusing, but there it is.

CHAPTER 18

I Persist

I PERSIST.

I don't seem to be able to give up. It seems I just can't.

Let me tell you the story of my pursuit of psychotherapy that illustrates my point.

I have been in therapy for 45 years. When I was 15 years old, I was living with Suzy and my younger sister in our new home after leaving the city where I had lived for most of my life. We were living in an apartment complex, an entirely new experience for me. From my birth until I was five, we had lived in the parsonage on the property that belonged to the church in Canada. We moved to the United States and lived in a rented house in a city in the Pacific Northwest in the Norwegian-American part of town. Bill was 100% Norwegian-American, so we went to the Lutheran Church where I learned to sing, at Christmas time, "*Dejlig er den Himmel blaa*," although, to be honest, I did not learn it in Norwegian. I learned to sing, "Bright and glorious is the sky." I did not learn to sing the carol in Norwegian until I went to a Lutheran college in 1980.

From the house in town, we moved to the northern part of the city, suburbia. So, finding myself living in an apartment complex where the population of residents had a much wider variety of lifestyles and values was a shock for me in 1975.

My understanding, now, of my inability to deal with the move to a new place and the people around me in the apartment complex, is informed by the knowledge I have today (which I did not have then) that I did not have a supportive parent. I recall that one night when Suzy was out drinking with some boyfriend, a child was crying on the other side of the wall that my bedroom shared with the bedroom in the next apartment. Even if Suzy had been home, I would not have asked her what to do. She was not supportive. The person who behaved like an adult in our household was, oftentimes, not Suzy. I was extremely upset to hear a child crying for more than half an hour with no one, apparently, responding. I knew the children next door. One of them was five years old, and the other was three years old.

I got out of bed, walked down the stairs, put my winter coat over my nightgown and opened my front door, planning to knock on the front door next door. However, I encountered the three-year-old girl standing in front of the front door crying loudly.

I picked her up, took her into her house, comforted her for about 20 minutes, put her to bed, and tucked her in. I read her a story and stayed in the room until she went to sleep. I talked to her brother, who told me that his mother was not home. I got him to sleep. I went downstairs and sat and waited for about an hour until their mother came back.

The mother, who knew me, of course, apologized for having caused me to have trouble with her children. She explained that she had just run down to the nearby store to get some cigarettes. I was 15 years old. I had no idea what to say or do. I had never been in a situation — not in my entire life — in which I was standing in front of an adult person who was blatantly lying to me.

I went home and went to bed. I don't remember if I even mentioned it to Suzy. If I did, she certainly did not teach me to call the appropriate children's protective agency.

Looking back, what I know, now, is that I was traumatized by this event. My childhood was a series of traumatizing events, and the absence of a parent to do parenting tasks is the reason. Distressing things happen to every fifteen-year-old person. But fifteen-year-old Jansen didn't even know that a young person ought to have someone to talk to or someone to turn to in such a situation. Young Jansen was under the impression that she (and everyone) was on her own — that this was simply how life was going to unfold.

It was during the time that the three of us were living in that apartment complex that I told Suzy that I needed to see a counselor. To her credit, she arranged for me to see a counselor. I recall going on a bus to see the counselor. I recall staying home from school some mornings and walking to the bus stop near the apartment complex to take the bus to the downtown area to see him.

I remember that I was no longer in control of my bowels by this time in my life. The horror of the life I was living caused my body to react by having episodes of painful diarrhea every day. It was not possible, in 1975, to buy diapers for adult-sized people in the grocery store. So, I ended up having poopy underwear quite often. I remember standing at that bus stop in front of the apartment complex wondering if it was worse to get on the bus and sit down, wondering if the feces would squish out and fall on the floor of the bus or if it was worse to go back to my apartment and clean up, which would mean that I would miss my appointment. Life was torture.

I will mention, parenthetically, that I saw that therapist for about six months until he asked my permission to speak to Suzy. I permitted him. I think he may have told Suzy that she was not being nice to me, because, after he met with Suzy, she did not allow me to see him again.

When I got to college, my persistence in seeking help through Western medicine began to show. I did not know that I was a person who engaged in self-harm. But I did hurt myself enough one day to feel frightened, and I went to Student Health and told them I needed to see a psychiatrist. The psychiatrist I was assigned was a stupid and scary person. I had enough sense to stop seeing him.

When I transferred to the Lutheran college, I went to the student support center and said I needed to see the counselor. I saw the counselor as often as they would allow during my two years in Minnesota.

I persisted in seeking Western-style mental health treatment when I moved to the city I now reside in, after my first foray into graduate school — a brief flirtation with a seminary in a different state. The therapist I saw first here was very supportive while I was deciding to get married and have a child, but not so helpful when I was deciding to put my two-year-old in daycare a few days a week and go back to school. I had to find a new therapist who would not need me to educate her about feminist ideas.

But that did not stop me from pursuing therapy. The next therapist had the traditional attitude toward borderline personality disorder. By traditional, I mean old-fashioned, *passé*. She was supportive while I got into graduate school as a student of computer science but then she sent me on my way because she did not want to have, in her practice, someone who was not going to get better! Some therapists do not wish to take on someone who will, in all truthfulness, need decades of therapy and whose profile suggests that they will be struggling nearly as much at the end of those decades as they were at the beginning.

(Some of you will be wondering if she told me that. No, she did not explicitly say so.)

It was about this time that I became a patient of the HMO that was not providing any kind of effective treatment. The therapy they were offering required a visit with your counselor that had to be completed before you could schedule another visit. The counselor's schedule (and this was in the 1990s) was filled on their calendar out to about six weeks in the future. So, one saw her therapist every six weeks. This is not therapy. This is pretend-therapy.

Lucky for me, I was married to someone who made a lot of money. I simply paid for my therapy during the 30 years that I was a member of that HMO.

When the HMO began to offer classes to teach skills for dealing with depression, I went to every class they offered me. After some time, Marcia Linehan's DBT came along. I participated in the HMO's DBT classes from the early days of their availability until the HMO referred me for treatment outside the HMO at a more sophisticated DBT clinic.

All this time, my suffering did not decrease at all.

Yet, I persisted.

All of this therapy was cognitive therapy. Almost all of it was working with these concepts: can I identify some thinking process in myself, which I have not been aware of, that leads me to make decisions or exhibit behaviors that are not to my advantage? Having identified some thought or thinking process that has been hidden to me that was probably useful in the past but does not help me now, what do I need to do to bring it into my conscious, everyday living? Now that it is part of my conscious thinking every day, do I want to change that way of thinking? What might I gain by changing it? What will I lose by changing it? How hard would it be to change? Am I that courageous? Am I ready to make that change? Leave me alone! Leave me alone! Leave me alone!

Well, that last part – "Leave me alone!" – that's not really part of cognitive therapy. That's just my commentary on cognitive therapy. Cognitive therapy is really hard. It's not fun at all. No one would do it if they didn't have to. Only when you're backed into a corner and things are terrible do you make these kinds of changes. (Unless you're a saint.)

So why did I persist? After all, **none of the cognitive therapy made me feel even one tiny bit better.**

I persisted because **the cognitive therapy did help me tidy up parts of my life that needed to get better.** My behavior got better. I came to be a person who had more choices. When I was interacting with human beings, I was able to look at a situation from more points of view, and I would see in front of me more choices than I used to be able to see.

So, the first reason I persisted was this: although there was no improvement in my pain, there was improvement in my behavior.

The second reason I persisted was that I had hope for improvement in the area of pain.

I am not certain that I still hold out any hope for improvement concerning my suffering. I have read a lot of research papers. Okay, that's not wholly true. I have read the abstracts of a lot of research papers. It appears to me that success in treating borderline personality disorder, if we set aside emergency psychiatric interventions, is measured by things that I don't care about. I care about a reduction in my suffering.

The abstracts of the research papers that I have seen seem to measure success in treating borderline personality disorder in terms of helping people with chaotic lives and troubles with suicide attempts move toward having more stable lives and be free of suicide attempts. (I'm sure that suicide attempts do nothing to contribute to a person's health and well-being.)

The abstract of a paper that is typical of the ones I see, this one published in the *American Journal of Psychiatry* [Bateman and Fonagy, 2008, doi.org/10.1176/appi.ajp.2007.07040636] gives the results of one study evaluating some patients, five years after discharge from a certain treatment, in terms of the patients' suicidality, diagnostic status, service use, use of medication, global function, and vocational status.

Notice that none of those is any measure of how the people feel. I guess service use may indicate something about the patients' suffering. If they are showing up at the emergency department frequently because they are in distress, perhaps in distress because they are worried that they will have a suicide attempt if they stay at home, that would indicate suffering. But, by itself, service use does not tell us a lot about their suffering.

The first paragraph of the paper itself is worth including here:

> *The natural course of borderline personality disorder and its long-term outcome following treatment are uncertain. A number of well-characterized treatments for borderline personality disorder have been found in randomized, controlled trials to reduce suicidal acts, self-harm, impulsive behaviors, general psychopathology, and service use while improving affective control. More limited evidence exists from these trials for changes in depression, loneliness/emptiness, anger, and social and interpersonal function with little confirmation of sustained improvement in any of these domains.*

Follow-up after treatment was either absent or too short to assess final outcomes.

Let me tell you what I think that means.

The first sentence, "The natural course of borderline personality disorder and its long-term outcome following treatment are uncertain" means we don't know much of anything about what happens to people with borderline personality disorder naturally or what happens to them if we treat them.

The second sentence, "A number of well-characterized treatments for borderline personality disorder have been found in randomized, controlled trials to reduce suicidal acts, self-harm, impulsive behaviors, general psychopathology, and service use while improving affective control" means some people have come up with really good treatments which we have studied. Our studies show that borderline patients who go through these treatments do have fewer suicide attempts and harm themselves less. They have fewer instances of impulsive behaviors, and they don't need as much care from our healthcare system. They also behave better.

The third sentence, "More limited evidence exists from these trials for changes in depression, loneliness/emptiness, anger, and social and interpersonal function with little confirmation of sustained improvement in any of these domains" means we have also studied these same really good treatments to see if people will be less depressed. We also want to know if borderline patients will stop feeling so lonely and empty. We were hoping they wouldn't be so angry and have so much trouble with other human beings. We found out that our studies didn't tell us very much at all about the borderline patients concerning depression and loneliness and anger. It looks like maybe the treatments that were very good for the suicide attempts and impulsive behaviors might've helped them a bit with the depression and loneliness and anger.

The fourth sentence, "Follow-up after treatment was either absent or too short to assess final outcomes" means we didn't check back with these borderline patients who had gone through treatment. We don't know what happened to them later. Well, we checked back with a few of them, but only after a couple of months or so. We didn't get organized to check back with them after one year and five years and ten years and fifteen years. So, we can't say anything useful about whether the treatments that are very good for reducing suicide attempts and impulsive behaviors in the short term are also very good for anything in the long term. Maybe they are. Maybe they are not. We just don't know.

As I said, this is a fairly standard group of statements about borderline personality disorder and treating borderline personality disorder. I haven't read anything that talks extensively about trying to measure whether people who are struggling with borderline personality disorder for years and years suffer less as the years go by.

I will admit to being quite discouraged. My quite-discouraged assessment is that researchers do not look into the question of suffering going down because suffering does not go down. My quite-discouraged assessment is that it would be like researching whether the pancreas of someone who has been insulin-dependent for 40 years has begun to make insulin again. If a person's pancreas stopped making all insulin when they were 10 years old, we know that it is not going to start making insulin when they are 50 years old. There would be no reason to do that research. Similarly, I fear, there is no reason to research to see if any treatment causes people with borderline personality disorder to suffer less. (I hope I'm wrong.)

Now I will finish my story about persisting. Since you know that I am quite discouraged, let me say again that I persist.

The HMO also offered me, repeatedly, the option of a partial hospitalization program. The phrase *partial hospitalization* is used to indicate that a person does not sleep overnight away from home but spends a significant part of her waking hours engaged with therapists and art therapists and psychiatrists and other professionals, both individually and in groups, working to get well. I participated in a three-week partial hospitalization program.

I did this during the time that my child was attending a private high school. I know I said that I homeschooled him — and I did. But Suzy became uncomfortable with the idea that he was not attending school at all. I forget what reason she gave. I had learned, at some point, not to listen to her very carefully. And I allowed her to contact schools and have them send me literature. One of the schools made it clear that parents would need to be comfortable with corporal punishment if their children were going to attend their school. That was, clearly, not going to be a good match!

There was, amongst the schools that sent literature, one that turned out to be a pretty good match for my child. It was a private school that was in its fifth year of operation. It had been founded by a woman who had worked in public schools for many years. She was passionate about her idea that the atmosphere of public schools was emotionally damaging to children. Her school had only 60 students in the four high school grades. Pretty much all of them were extremely smart, and all of them were either artists or computer nerds. Since my child had never been exposed to a group of people who would have told him that he was somehow unacceptable because of his interest in computers and books and staying indoors to do things like play computer games, he did not know that some parts of our culture would consider him to be defective. (Or, perhaps I should say, I hope he did not.)

His attendance at school allowed me to persist in an even more persistent manner with work on getting well from my psychiatric troubles. I branched out into non-Western medicine. I found a fine acupuncturist.

A time came when the person who is now my ex-husband changed jobs, and the HMO was no longer an option. For the first time in my adult life, I was covered by insurance that was not managed-care. I needed to find a psychiatrist, and it happened that the best psychiatrist I had ever had in the HMO had left the HMO and was practicing in town. I arranged to see her and found that she also was doing psychodynamic psychotherapy. So, for the first time, I had a psychiatrist as my therapist.

She was charging more than $600 per session, and I saw her four times per week. My therapy bill was more than $10,000 per month. Insurance paid quite a bit of that, but not all of it.

I also established a relationship with a therapist who had expertise in working with the body. I knew that I needed to begin to address my inability to experience certain physical sensations.

That is my story of persistence in the area of psychotherapy. There are many other therapists I saw along the way whom I did not mention. Sometimes a therapist is a bad match, and the relationship has to be ended. Sometimes a therapist becomes ill and stops practicing. I have had a therapist leave town. For many reasons, it becomes necessary to search, yet again, for a new therapist. Yikes!

I persist.

I could write this chapter again about persisting with finding appropriate medications for my skin and doctors for my skin and clothing for my skin. I persist with my skin. Or I could write this chapter again about getting the homeowners' association to exhibit good behavior toward me regarding my property or my neighbor who is harassing me or the minutes of the meetings at which I spoke in which I am misquoted or their bad behavior toward mentally ill people in our neighborhood. I persist with the homeowners' association. There are many other possibilities for alternate chapters also.

I persist.

As much as I like to point out how Suzy damaged me, I have to admit that I learned to persist from Suzy. She was an incredibly strong person. She used to say she was going to live to be 100 years old. If she could have lived to be 100 by force of will, she would have lived to be 100. When she decided to do something, she did it. Nothing would stop her.

She did not care who said that she could not do something. She did not believe anybody who said she could not do something. If she thought she could do it, then she could do it.

She was 5 feet tall and weighed 104 pounds, but she would lift anything, move anything, go anywhere, do anything.

She was amazingly foolish in the things that she would do. She would do things that would almost get her killed, do them because she decided she could. She was crazy. But you could not tell her that she could not do anything.

Suzy grew two inches taller when she got to college. It was the first time in her life she had had enough food to eat. I am guessing that it was also the first time in her life that she had felt at all safe. People don't grow when they don't have food. And people don't grow, even if they have food, if they are terrified.

Then Suzy earned an undergraduate degree. Then she earned a master's degree. Then she got a divorce. Then she got another divorce. Then she stopped marrying stupid men.

Suzy was not a person who should've been anybody's mother. But she was one brave person! No one was going to tell her to crawl in a hole and die. I persist partly because Suzy persisted, and I am her daughter.

I, too, persist.

CHAPTER 19
I Am an Excellent Problem-Solver

I AM SURPRISED I am still alive.

I doubt that persons who are suffering from borderline personality disorder at the level of severity that I suffer are usually alive at age 60. When I consider that I have four other mental illness diagnoses and I consider the severity of my skin problem, I can see why psychiatrists and therapists are often amazed that I am alive.

It is less common for people whom I meet in my day-to-day life to be amazed that I am alive. I present well. That is, my presentation of myself to the world is indistinguishable from that of a 60-year-old woman in the middle class and in the mainline culture of the United States who has no particular unusual features. Well, perhaps my haircut is slightly unusual. I have very short hair, short like a man's short haircut, above my ears and curls on top of my head, then some long hair in the back. My hair is naturally strawberry blonde, now mixed with gray. That's about it for unusual features.

In fact, people sometimes don't want to believe that I have had anything unusual happen to me. One of the most damaging interactions I have with human beings is the strange experience of talking to people about my conviction that I had a seriously abusive childhood and am living a life of intense suffering and having them react as if I am a whiner and a complainer.

There is a behavior I want to discuss that is so common that it has a name: **blaming the victim**. There are several reasons that people exhibit the behavior of blaming the victim — the reasons are widely different. However, blaming the victim always has the feature that the person who is experiencing something negative is told that he or she could escape the negative experience if he or she would just be different or act differently. The message is sent directly or subtly that the sufferer is at fault for the suffering.

This is one of the most damaging interactions I have with human beings. I long to tell someone about the horror of my childhood experiences, but when I do, I sometimes get an answer such as, "I think you misunderstand what your mother was saying in that case. Everyone's parents make mistakes."

There is a suitcase full of blaming the victim in these two sentences.

First, the person speaking is suggesting that the child, not the mother, was at fault in the long-ago interaction. Little Jansen was to blame.

Next, the person speaking is suggesting that the present-day Jansen, who is opening her heart and speaking about pain, is creating her pain by thinking the wrong thoughts.

Not far under the surface of those two sentences lies the idea that present-day Jansen could stop suffering if she would understand what her mother had said long ago and understand it correctly, then recognize that her mother, like everyone's mother, had made a mistake. Just think the right thoughts and you won't suffer!

This mini-lecture blames the victim: Jansen is the victim of suffering. Jansen is suffering. Jansen can fix it. Therefore, Jansen is responsible for her suffering.

Sometimes, blaming the victim is motivated by the kindest of intentions. Not wishing to see Jansen suffer, the speaker may be sincerely offering what they see as a clear and easy way to escape the unpleasantness. But really! Can we ever hand to another person an easy way to escape anything?

Blaming the victim can also be motivated by something less kind. An unconscious (or even conscious) desire to get someone to stop talking about their suffering can motivate blaming the victim.

More often, a need to pretend that suffering just does not happen, especially to someone we care about, motivates a gentle blaming of the victim that so many of us know, from experience, usually has the effect of suppressing any heartfelt conversation. Thank goodness! That deep sharing is over! Let's talk about the weather, for goodness sake.

I'll omit other types of blaming the victim which are even darker.

Now I come to my point: there is no need to blame me for much of anything. I am an excellent problem-solver. I am not a person who turns away from problems. I do not ignore problems. If something can be approached as if it is a problem — a problem that can be solved algorithmically, step-by-step, with actions taken in the real world by the use of a computer or a pen or my voice or a car — I tackle those things with enthusiasm and courage and competence and almost always with success.

There are things for which I deserve blame. However, I am an excellent problem-solver; so, I seldom deserve the blame for failing to pay a bill or failing to find a therapist or failing to take my medications. I do not forget an appointment. If it is incumbent upon me to learn the difference between a 401(k) and an IRA, I can do that quickly and well. If my next car is electric and not a gasoline user, I will learn whether it can or cannot jumpstart another car. I can solve problems.

I get things done because I can solve problems. I get jobs. I earn degrees. I get my child into schools. I get money for things I want to do. I find the best deal on certain kinds of airplane tickets. I don't get fooled by scams. I know the difference between one kind of elastic and another. I know which kind of audiobooks will play on my car's sound system. If it has an answer in the area of information, I can find the answer.

This is probably the reason I'm still alive. When I become dysregulated, that is, extremely upset, I do not exhibit the same kind of behavior that creates a chaotic life so many borderline people have. I don't gamble away my money or impulsively quit a job. I seem to be a problem-solver rather than a problem-creator.

Suzy may be largely the reason for this skill, just as she was, to a great degree, the reason for my persistence.

In some situations, however, Suzy was a horrible problem-solver, so I had to become a good problem-solver. Navigating on highways, for example, she was a terror. I recall that we would be driving along with my older sister in the passenger seat and my younger sister and me in the back seats. I was called upon to look at the highway signs because I could see farther than any of the others. Suzy would be trying to drive us to someplace she had chosen. She would be saying, "I don't know where I'm supposed to get off the freeway. Am I supposed to get off here? Or is it the next exit? Should I get off here? Where should I get off?"

I was the most sensitive of the three daughters — sensitive in the sense that I picked up on her needs very quickly and had the best ability to deliver the most advantageous response immediately. I had learned that the frantic freeway frenzy required an immediate answer delivered with great confidence. It was more important to give a decisive answer than to be correct. Consequently, I would authoritatively say, "Take this exit!"

I had figured out, over the years, that it did not especially matter if I was wrong. Suzy was in such a frenzied state that she could not track what had happened, step-by-step. The fact that I sometimes gave her the wrong answer, and gave it with confidence, was forgotten in her confusion over trying to get to our destination. She did not blame me; she did not blame anyone. Indeed, if she were to blame me for being wrong, she would have to take the blame herself for being wildly incompetent. She was, in fact, wildly incompetent when she took us on these outings.

(The outings were frequently terrifying because we would be there on the wrong day or she would forget the tickets or it would be something completely inappropriate for children or it would be something truly not safe.)

Eventually, I was cast in the role of problem-solver in the family. "We have only eight dollars until the end of the month," Suzy told me once when I was 14 years old. I remember this incident because no amount of sensitivity or creativity provided me with any clue to an appropriate response. I did not know what kind of problem-solving I could possibly do for her at that moment.

I had to be extremely careful — if I sounded too controlling or competent, she would see through the charade and snap at me saying, "I am the mother, here!" If I expressed compassion for her anxiety, I had to do it extremely carefully. If I seemed too compassionate, she would snap at me, saying, "I'm not worried about this!"

What I did not know was that other teenagers did not spend hours each day trying to solve their parent's problems and scheming about how to present their solutions in just the right words so that they would not be punished. I did all of this while I succeeded in high school well enough to get into a prestigious university, succeeded on the speech team earning trophies for my Winnie the Pooh interpretive speeches, continued my not-voluntary training as a classical cellist, sewed clothing for myself as my only artistic expression, participated in the student government and all those other things that bright, young scholars are expected to do.

Occasionally I see someone wearing a T-shirt that says, "I can do anything: I am a mom!" Perhaps someday it will be okay to wear a T-shirt saying, "I can do anything: my parents are profoundly narcissistic!" Actually, what we need to do is sell T-shirts for one dollar each so that they are easily available to teenagers and have them say, "I can do anything: I am the only competent person at my house. Get me out of there! (I'm not kidding. Call children's protective services right now.)"

That's the T-shirt I should have been wearing. Yet, even without it, I am still alive at 60…surprisingly.

CHAPTER 20
I Observe My Own Behavior

MY VERY FIRST recollection of observing my own behavior comes from kindergarten.

I remember that the stalls in the bathroom in the building where I went to kindergarten had no doors, and I remember I was not the very lowest girl on the social pecking order.

This is the memory: three girls were standing with their backs to a wall and facing a toilet stall. Sitting on the toilet in that stall was the girl who had the unfortunate place at the bottom of the pecking order. The girls were pointing at her and saying something about being able to see her genitals. (I don't remember what words they were using. The children I grew up with must have come from homes that did not use strong language or didn't use strong language in front of children, because I think the girls were saying that they could see this child's bottom.)

Because the year was 1965, we little girls were wearing dresses to school. I remember observing that I had draped my dress down over my knees as I was sitting on the toilet to protect myself from comments from these girls. My five-year-old mind was wondering why the child nearby was so foolish as to fail to do the same.

The public school provided me with many opportunities to observe the behavior of other people and to observe my behavior. To protect myself, I became quite good at being able to notice what I was doing. The protection resulted from noting what I was doing, comparing my actions (or words) to those of people who had more safety than me, deciding if I wanted to make a change, and then, sometimes, changing what I was doing.

I was able to blend in well enough that I was physically safe almost all the time. I was assaulted only once at school, and that time I did not suffer any serious injury to my body when a classmate put me in a headlock after learning that I, and not he, had gotten the highest score on a physics test.

Safety in other places has been another advantage of being able to observe my behavior and modify it. Many have been the times that I have been afraid and have needed to monitor my posture and gait to do my best not to telegraph my fear.

My ability to observe my behavior and modify it may spring from an unfortunate source. Children who live in a home that does not provide them with safety become hypervigilant. Although I was not beaten, my home was not safe; it was not emotionally safe. I was emotionally abandoned regularly. I was emotionally attacked in ways that were extremely subtle — and that happened every day. Threats were present every time I had to be near anyone in my home.

Children become hypervigilant because they need to survive. Little Jansen learned to pay attention to every movement of Suzy's hands and face so that she, little Jansen, could make the very best guess about what Suzy would want next. My survival as a small child (and even as a bigger child) depended upon guessing well what to do to please Suzy.

Everyone was expected to know just exactly what to do. If Suzy had to put her desires into words, everyone who was at home at the time had already failed. It was expected that her wishes would be carried out without needing any spoken requests from her. She truly believed that the world was full of tools that ought to be doing what she wanted.

This hypervigilance I made into an ability to observe myself and make myself into whatever was most advantageous at any moment. This is both absolutely crazy and a huge advantage for survival. Hence, I am both absolutely crazy…and still alive.

I think that those statements need further explication:

Please, forgive me for saying I am absolutely crazy. Please, don't misunderstand. The word "crazy" carries with it many negative connotations. I would not use that word to describe someone other than myself.

Similarly, I describe myself as "fat." It does not bother me to say that I am fat. For me, the word means that I weigh a lot. Somebody else who is the same height as I am might weigh substantially less and still be perfectly healthy. But, I would not describe someone else as fat. Right now, in our culture, in the United States in 2020, to say someone is fat is to say something bad about them. So, I will take the word "fat" for myself; I will not use the word "fat" for someone else.

I am okay with the word "crazy." I use it about myself only in limited circumstances. I would not say, in general, that I am crazy. I do say that I am mentally ill. I believe that is a statement about me that is generally true. Quite a lot of Jansen Vee is mentally ill. Just as someone might be diabetic and would describe their entire self as "diabetic," not just their pancreas, I feel that my whole self is mentally ill. But I do not think that all of me is crazy.

The process that occurred through no one's fault, by which I grew up in a home where I was not safe and I became hypervigilant, allowing me to observe myself and make myself into whatever is most advantageous at the moment, is both absolutely crazy and a huge advantage for survival. As a result, some part of me is absolutely crazy and I am still alive.

It's pretty bad, pretty crazy really, to be so able to morph into whatever is most advantageous at the moment. Sometimes this is called the "chameleon effect." It can be so pronounced for some borderline personality disorder patients that they can have a set of acquaintances in one realm, say at church, and a set of acquaintances in another realm, say at work, and could not imagine encountering both sets at the same time. This patient is very much a different person at church than at work.

I have not suffered from the chameleon effect to that degree. However, I have no idea who the real Jansen is. I don't know what kind of food I would like if I had not been influenced by 33 years of marriage. I don't know what kind of activities I would like if I could have chosen for myself. I don't know what kind of subjects I would have studied or what kind of career I might have pursued. I can observe my behavior and change it so easily that I have no idea what I might really want to do!

The other day, I was chatting with a friend who was telling me how hard it is to get help for her son at her son's public school. Her son is academically extremely successful. Because he can do so many wonderful things with his very good thinking mind, she has difficulty getting the attention of any of the professionals at the public school for his needs. He is not needing help with his academics — but he needs help in some other areas. It's almost as if he is not allowed to have any needs because he is so smart.

At the risk of seeming like I should not be allowed to complain, I want to say that it can be a problem for me that I'm good at so many things. It is hard to know what direction to take in life — it is hard to know what the real Jansen might like to do or want to do — when I am a good musician and a good programmer and a good artist and a good teacher and a good nurturer of children and a good writer and a good designer of curricula and a good decorator and a good designer of clothing and good seamstress. I make bras; I am qualified to home-school a child from kindergarten until ready for MIT; I build play structures; I write liturgies; I do my own braids and dreadlocks; I make my own cheese and meat alternatives; I solder and am a competent user of electronics meters; I replace breakers in my electrical panel; I rein-stall Windows 10 when needed; I know how to use my winches safely; I fix my appliances; I knit my socks.

Sometimes I tell people I do everything except weld. But that's not true. I'm allergic to plants and animals. So, I don't raise any food. Having so many skills and the ability to learn new skills, I feel almost like a person who is a piece of cloth made up not of a pattern of reds and oranges but a person who is a many-colored plaid.

In summary, the upside of observing my own behavior and modify-ing it has been safety and fitting in. The downside has been a lack of knowledge of who Jansen really is. But there's still time. I am always trying to get to know Jansen.

What color is a chameleon? What color when it is resting on a plaid?

Who am I? What am I? Despite my continual self-observation, I only wish I knew.

CHAPTER 21
I Analyze All Kinds of Things

MY MIND IS busy analyzing all day long — all the time. I can analyze all kinds of things. This gift has contributed significantly to my survival.

I think mathematically. Let me give you an example. I was listening to someone talking about teaching children to recognize patterns. As is sometimes done for grade school children (or adults), a number pattern puzzle was presented as a single number input into a mysterious box. The mysterious box would then send out some number as an answer.

The mysterious box, we were told, took the input of two and sent out the answer four. The mysterious box took the input of three and sent out the answer six. The presenter gave us only those two examples, and she then proceeded to discuss how to teach children patterns, how people learn patterns, why patterns are important, and her experience with teaching patterns.

I didn't hear much of the presenter's words after the mysterious box had processed its two inputs to get two outputs. Mathematically, we would express that as number pairs (2, 4) and (3, 6), and we could plot them as two points on an x-y graph (x,y). My mind was distracted wondering if the presenter believed that we knew what the mysterious box did when it got a number. Did she think that we were now prepared to act as does the mysterious box? If I wanted to be the mysterious box, and the input number was four, did the presenter imagine that I knew what the output number ought to be? **Any formula** that produced a curve that passed through these two points, (2, 4) and (3, 6), on the x-y graph would be correct.

I was a bit disappointed: the larger topic of the discussion was mathematics. Teaching patterns is a part of mathematics. But patterns, themselves, are also part of mathematics. I was stuck on the pattern, and I could not think about teaching patterns while I was distracted by the pattern itself.

Not only that, I knew there was more than one pattern that could accept a two as input and give a four as output while it, the very same pattern, accepted a three is input and gave a six as output. One of those patterns is a doubling pattern. But another one of those patterns, if you graph it on a piece of paper, makes the shape of a parabola. Again, any curve that joined the two points would be correct with the information given so far, not exclusively y = 2x.

As soon as the thought of a parabola that passes through the points (2, 4) and (3, 6) came into my mind, there was pretty much no hope of my listening to the presenter anymore. I was much more interested in knowing the equation of the parabola that passes through those two points. And, oh, my goodness! There are two of those in 2-space! One opens upward. One opens downward.

This is how my mind works. I analyze everything all the time.

Sometimes I wonder how I survived childhood despite being provided with almost no intellectual stimulation. In my family of origin, people did not discuss ideas. I never saw either of my parents reading a book. Although I was taken to the library in the summer, and Suzy gets credit for that, I was not introduced to nonfiction reading.

Neither of my parents learned anything of an intellectual nature for their enjoyment during the time I lived in their homes. Although they played cards with Suzy's side of the family, and this required very keen minds, they did not play cards with the children. At the dinner table, there was no discussion of current events that I can remember.

I do recall being lucky enough to go with my mother to the university bookstore when she went to buy her graduate school textbooks one term. I bravely asked her to buy me a Norwegian language textbook and an algebra textbook. Surprisingly, she did so. However, she did not take it upon herself to make an effort to get me instruction in Norwegian language or mathematics.

I recall reading that algebra textbook over and over again. Having no one to tell me why there were letters in the math book (I was about eight years old, so I had only seen numbers in math), I did not succeed at teaching myself. It would never have occurred to me to ask either of my parents for help. My parents were not people I could turn to for help with anything.

Things are different now. I have plenty of things to think about and analyze today. What I lack now is some context, some group of friends or colleagues, amongst whom to be my real self with this mind that has these analytical thoughts. If I were not so severely and persistently mentally ill, I think I would have had a career as a researcher or teacher in academia. In such a context, I believe my mind would not seem so unusual.

This ability to analyze all kinds of things has kept me alive. I don't think I could be alive if I did not spend a lot of time wondering what is happening to me. I wonder:

1. What is this experience I just had?
2. Is this thing, which I just did, a normal thing or a mental illness thing?
3. Do normal people (whatever "normal" means) have that behavior I just exhibited? Or not?
4. Was it noticeable that I just acted in a manner motivated by my mental illness?
5. Do I need to do something to compensate for the fact that I just acted in a manner motivated by my mental illness?
6. If I take an action now because my just-completed action was strange and possibly scary to someone, is it likely to make things better? Or make things worse?
7. Is this person to whom I am speaking reacting to me as if I am a normal person (again, whatever "normal" means), or have I revealed that I have a severe and persistent mental illness? Is it important?
8. Is this a situation in which I wish to try to blend in? Is there any reason to hide my mental illness at this time?
9. Am I becoming strident or unrealistically insistent on getting my way? That is, could it be the case that the emotions I do not have access to are getting in my way and causing me a problem right now?

These are things I wonder about "in the moment," so to speak. But I also analyze things in larger arcs:

1. Over the past year, is my self-care deteriorating?
2. Is my suicidal ideation becoming more intense?

3. Or falling off?
4. Is this current therapist helping me?
5. Or do I find myself wishing I did not have to go to therapy today?
6. In the past five years, have I made any friends?
7. Have I alienated more people than I have befriended?
8. How many decisions in the past 10 years would I go back and change, if I could?

I have heard that some people need to set aside a day once a week to be their Sabbath day, or they set aside a week once a year for a retreat to remember to make these kinds of bigger questions part of their life. I think about these things routinely. Perhaps I think about them too much. I'm not sure.

Continual analysis has kept me alive because I always have some idea of what is happening to me and what I need to do to make my life better. Even if I am completely wrong about what is happening to me and completely wrong about what will make my life better, at least I never have the attitude that someone else is the expert who knows what is happening to me and someone else had better tell me how to make my life better.

I am more than self-directed — I am passionately devoted to being in charge of myself. I may not know very much about who Jansen is, but no one is going to tell me that they are the expert on Jansen. I spend a lot of time thinking about what **is** happening to me and what **could** happen to me and what **did** happen to me. No one else has spent that much time and energy trying to figure out Jansen.

Furthermore, it has been quite helpful to try to figure out Suzy. It has also been quite helpful to try to figure out Bill. And it has been quite helpful to try to figure out the environment in which I was an infant and later a small child with Suzy and Bill and the other two girls.

Suzy was very smart and very damaged. In her later years, she did consult a psychiatrist, from time to time, when she was especially troubled. Mostly, she was especially troubled when she was angry with her daughters.

After Suzy died, I went to see her psychiatrist, and my two sisters joined us at his office by telephone. This doctor opened the meeting with a question made in a tone of voice that showed that he was prepared to stick up for Suzy, whom he viewed as a wronged mother. He asked us, "Do you three women know that your mother didn't trust you?"

I was surprised, but not very surprised. My lack of surprise came from being fully aware that Suzy felt that I was an inadequate daughter. She would say, right in front of me, "Everyone who was supposed to love me has abandoned me!"

My element of surprise stemmed from this being a psychiatrist speaking the words. He had only the words he had heard from Suzy upon which to form his opinion of the relationships among Suzy and her three daughters. Amazingly, he had been completely taken in by Suzy!

Suzy had told him what terrible daughters we were, and he had not imagined that he was hearing this from a patient who was speaking about her deep feelings rather than relating the literal truth. This psychiatrist did not begin the meeting by saying, "It was so unfortunate that your mother had mixed feelings about you." He did not say, "I can imagine that it was painful to have your mother, at times, think that you were harming her." No, Suzy was so smart and so good at presenting her position as the truth that she had taken him in completely — a psychiatrist.

My older sister, when as a teenager she reached the age of having a driver's license, fantasized about stealing the family station wagon, bundling me and my younger sister into the car, and driving us away to freedom and safety. She longed to do it. She yearned to do it. I have heard her talk about it; I have seen her weep 40 years later about not accomplishing that rescue.

But Suzy was so smart and so good at presenting her position as the truth that my older sister knew that we would get caught and we would be brought back. Then, Suzy would present her truth; my sister would present her truth; the teenager would look like a lying, irresponsible person; Suzy would look like the perfect mother; things would be even worse than before. So, the teenager never acted out her fantasy rescue.

It has been helpful to figure out Bill. In the Vee family, hierarchy is supremely important. Bill was a son, and he was the oldest of the children. He was a minister. Therefore, he was good by definition. I am not sure Bill could conceive of himself doing anything bad. I am fairly certain his siblings could not conceive of his doing anything bad. When Bill died of cancer at age 68, his only living parent died 10 weeks later. Coincidence?

Despite being my father, Bill did not want to take care of me. He was afraid of me. He was afraid that, somehow, he would get tricked into taking care of me or taking care of my son. He once said to me, out of the blue, "I am so glad you are raising your son. So many of my friends are having to raise their grandchildren."

Think of that! Contrast that with some other grandfather saying that he would want his daughter to know that if she should die, he would, of course, take care of that little grandbaby. Of course, he would. Not Bill. He was thanking me for raising my own child.

It has been helpful to me to understand the family I grew up in. Now that I understand that I was on edge all the time, fearing the next subtle emotional attack at any moment, I know that the seemingly calm family was not a safe family. I would guess that 80% of the people who are raised in this kind of emotionally abusive family go to their graves without having any idea that anything bad had happened to them. I know that Bill would never have guessed that he and his family were emotionally abusive. But it is almost certain that he was raised in an environment where no one was attentive to his emotional needs. And clearly, no one was attentive to Suzy's emotional needs (or even her physical needs).

If I had not been able to analyze all kinds of things, I would not have been able to provide my child with so many skills that he could not learn just by picking them up from others. My child is on the autism spectrum. It is simply second nature for me to notice that a child needs to learn something. I am a teacher at heart; I see a need and I jump in and teach.

If I had not been able to analyze all kinds of things, I would not have been able to notice that my husband, now my former husband, was actually unkind, even though he does not yell or hit. For 20 years of our 33-year marriage, I was certain that someone who did not yell at me or hit me was kind. However, eventually, I began to be more mentally healthy and my analytical mind began to tell me that it simply could not be the case that it was kind behavior when he stood in the grocery store and argued with me, saying that I could not have the 10-pound bag of flour that I wanted; I had to buy two 5-pound bags of flour. Why? Two 5-pound bags of flour cost a total of $0.22 less than one 10-pound bag of flour. He would have stood there and argued forever! He was immovable. I was not worth an extra $0.22.

I will continue to survive, not just because of the ability to analyze all kinds of things, but also because of the other peculiar gifts that I have: I talk despair, but I act hope; I persist; I am an excellent problem-solver; I have an unusual ability to observe my behavior.

Of course, I will not survive forever — each of us will die. My hope is not to die directly as the result of being mentally ill, but to die in a more everyday manner.

I believe there is something so important about human beings that the death of our bodies is not the whole story. Throughout time and around the world, many people have had some kind of sense that human beings are precious and special in a way that death cannot destroy. I do not expect to be destroyed by death.

I believe there is something stronger than death and that it defeats death in the end.

I believe that after my death, I will continue to be engaged with that strong thing, differently and more intensely.

Until then, I will survive.

CHAPTER 22
So, Am I Mentally Ill? Or Not?

TWO THINGS ARE clear: first, a great many unfortunate things have occurred in my life, and second, I have some wonderful qualities that have allowed me to survive.

Is it useful for me to describe myself as mentally ill? I repeat, is it useful?

Let's not ask the question, "Is Jansen mentally ill?" That question is more profound than the question, "Is it useful for me to describe myself as mentally ill?"

If we want to determine whether I **am** mentally ill, we move quickly towards existential and ontological questions — that is, questions that delve into what it is to exist and what is the very nature of being.

It is for this reason that sensitive people do not say, "Look, there is a disabled person," but they have trained themselves to say, instead, "… a person with a disability."

Do you see the difference? In the first case, the **entire person** is being called a disabled person. In the second case, a person is being identified and then, secondarily, the fact that they have a disability is being brought to our attention.

Sometimes, people poke fun at this small change in words because it seems so petty and nitpicking. However, if you care to be amongst the ranks of sensitive people, I would advise you not to poke fun at any language distinctions that seem to be petty and nitpicking unless you are in the group that is insisting on the language distinctions.

There was a time when saying that somebody was "retarded" was the polite term to avoid saying that they were an idiot. Perhaps, if you are not 60 years old or older, you do not recall a time when referring to a human being as "retarded" was polite. But I assure you, it was. Language distinctions come and go. They are not insignificant.

So here is my language distinction: rather than asking if I **am** mentally ill let's ask if it is useful for me to describe myself as mentally ill. Yes, for me, in my case, speaking only for myself, I find it useful to describe myself as mentally ill. There are benefits and there are drawbacks to saying that I am mentally ill. I choose to describe myself that way.

My language distinction (describing myself as mentally ill rather than saying I am mentally ill) is not especially workable. I violated it, in fact, in the above paragraph. Oh, I wish that human language were as neat and tidy as the mathematics that I so enjoyed teaching to college students. I used to teach symbolic logic to undergraduate students in their second year of a computer science major. Symbolic logic can express some things very precisely. But the range of things it can express is limited.

I reap the **benefits** of describing myself as mentally ill in the areas of obtaining health care, obtaining services, and having an effective shorthand for communicating information. I suffer the **drawbacks** of describing myself as mentally ill because of the stigma still associated with mental illness.

A young woman I know, a generation younger than I am, came into my life at a time when she believed that taking psychotropic medications or talking to a psychotherapist would change her into a different person. She did not want to obtain health care for the suffering she was enduring. She recognized that it was suffering; she recognized that it was emotional suffering; she recognized that Western medicine, at this time, would steer her toward medication and therapy; she was not interested.

I do not know this woman well, but I do know she made friends with several people who were comfortable with mental illness as a medical condition. All of them had a scientific approach to medicine — that is, they were heavily invested in Western medicine. They viewed the brain as an organ that can have chemical imbalances as well as structural problems (not to mention other conditions and configurations) which are classified as mental illness. As this woman became familiar with this manner of assessing some aspects of suffering and also found out that some people she respected had taken advantage of medication and therapy, she softened in her stance. Well, I do not have any idea why she came to be more open to the ideas of medication and therapy. I cannot speak for her. I only know that she did eventually consider medication and therapy.

I am always pleased to see people consider medication and therapy. Both medication and psychotherapy have been helpful to me. I should add that neither medication nor psychotherapy seems to have the power to prevent the intense suffering that may lead me to a suicide death. I am not sure what prevents people from going ahead with medication and psychotherapy to relieve that suffering which can be addressed with those tools. I suspect it is the same kind of resistance that I saw in myself when my blood pressure began to go up.

I am fully aware that my blood pressure would probably be at an acceptable level if I could return to the habits I had 15 years ago: going to the gym five days a week, engaging in work that I feel is valuable to society, getting enough sleep, and eating healthier food than I am eating now. So, after my self-care drastically and suddenly fell off from quite good to quite poor and my blood pressure went up, I resisted taking a medication that would bring down my blood pressure. I explained to my doctor that I knew I needed to reform my self-care. I negotiated with her to give me three months to get my self-care under control.

At the end of three months, I was still unable to face the fact that I was not able to eat well and exercise. Even though I know that I am facing tremendous challenges that do not allow me to take good care of myself at this time, I still refused to take the blood pressure medication. I was not in danger of having a stroke immediately, but I was not healthy. It took me another few months before I consented to take the medication, and now I am on two blood-pressure-controlling medications.

I confess to feeling that I am a failure because I have to take blood-pressure-controlling medications. Does that make sense? I am doing the right thing for my blood pressure. It would be foolish to refuse to take these medications. The reality of my life is that I need to take these medications. I am doing what is wise and healthful for me. Yet, somehow I feel that I am not completely successful in my life because I am taking these medications. This is silly, in a way.

Yet, this is typical of how the human mind works. I am sure many feel that, somehow, taking medication to control, say, anxiety indicates a failure of some sort. I can imagine that somebody might think, just as I think about my blood pressure, that they ought to be able to take care

167

of their anxiety without medication. Never mind that they actually cannot do so! Never mind that it is wise and healthful to take the anxiety medication! Swallowing that pill might make them feel somehow as if they are not quite good enough. This is silly, in a way.

Yet, this is typical of how the human mind works.

I have overcome the feeling that mental illness in myself is any indication of failure.

Part of overcoming the stigma of mental illness, for me, has been understanding that I do not wake up in the morning and say to myself, "I think I shall suffer as much as possible today."

It is not part of my plan to have difficulty connecting with other human beings. I do not scheme about ways to feel that I do not deserve to have a place on Earth. When I purchase food, I do not use my imagination to envision that every bite I put in my mouth will feel like the last bite of food I will ever get, so that I will be distressed every time I eat anything.

All of this suffering comes to me without any action that I take. It just comes to me. It has no source from any person or entity. The suffering emerged from the confluence of some horribly unfortunate events.

Understanding that no one is at fault has permitted me to begin small steps of self-compassion. I wish I could report giant leaps of self-compassion, but I find self-compassion to be terrifying. Every tiny gain I make in the area of self-compassion requires admitting, just a little bit more, how bad things have been.

That means giving up denial.

Denial is a powerful coping mechanism. Denial is a perfectly acceptable coping mechanism. I do not fault anyone for coping through denial, unless that denial is harming some human person. I would guess that the vast majority of people who were raised in homes like the home created by Suzy and Bill have no idea that any emotional abuse occurred in their past. Denial is keeping that realization at bay.

If this allows them to live some kind of happy life, and they are not harming anyone, maybe that's okay. I am not certain that they could avoid harming anyone, but I might entertain that notion.

I feel I must be careful not to break open maliciously someone's denial simply for my own reasons. When someone's ability to deny their suffering is removed, they often encounter a crisis. I try not to induce a crisis in anyone unless it is important to protect some vulnerable person and, also, I must I feel I can stick around and nurture the person through the crisis. Otherwise, it is not ethical to break into someone's denial.

(I do, however, report child abuse to the authorities. I call the police when I hear someone beating someone in a house nearby. I call the Educational Services District when I know a child is not receiving appropriate services. Rarely is it my job to do the work, directly, of protecting a vulnerable person. Normally, I use the systems which we have that are set up to do so.)

My willingness to state that I am struggling with mental illness allows me to get coverage from my health insurance for therapy and medications. I have been less successful at getting my county to provide me with services in my home to help with dishes and laundry, bathing, and other self-care tasks. Currently, in the county in which I live, help is available only if one is physically incapable of doing these tasks. Being incapacitated because of the symptoms of mental illness — having, for example, only two or three good hours per day — does not qualify a person for help in the home. This is true even though I receive a disability income from the federal government.

The sentence, "I struggle with mental illness," also provides me with a shorthand, so to speak, useful for communicating to people in a pithy manner my challenges. Although "mental illness" covers a huge range of symptoms and troubles, to tell someone that I struggle with mental illness tells them enough that they can be prepared for me to be a person who has more to deal with, perhaps, than the challenges of everyday life. It also signals that some unusual behavior may emerge. They have been warned, alerted.

The question of unusual behavior is a little bit difficult. Quite a lot of mental illness comes with no unusual behavior at all. Depression comes to mind. Depression is the common cold of mental illness. Depression does not cause any unusual behavior. Possibly, a depressed person might weep a little more easily than someone else. However, a depressed person would not lose control of the ability to desist from weeping in a social setting. To be depressed is not to be out of control. Indeed, to be mentally ill is not to be out of control.

In my case, mental illness does come with some unusual behavior. When my PTSD is triggered, the entire intensity of a lifetime of trauma is suddenly in my in-this-moment experience. As an example, let me tell you about a time that I was walking through the Fellowship Hall at church during a church service. I had left the worship service because I had decided I wanted some coffee. Glancing out the window at the playground, I saw a child, about age 2, standing on the playground, barefoot although it was February and 40° outside. No coat.

I did not see any parent with this child. However, I could not see the whole playground, so I got my coffee and went to use the bathroom. But as I was walking back toward the sanctuary, I saw that the child was still standing in the very same spot. He was not playing; he was just standing still.

I stepped out the door and said hello. It was not a child I recognized. He did not answer, so I told him my name and asked him if he had come to church with his parents or his grandparents. He did not move a muscle or answer. I asked him if he was interested in having a cookie (even though I knew that children are taught these days not to take sweets from a stranger). Then, receiving no answer, I told him that I was going to sit down on a nearby bench.

I sat down on the bench and talked to him about this and that. I tried my limited amount of Spanish. "Puedo decir, mi perro blanco se llama Daisy." "Necessito piñata." I got no different reaction to my silly Spanish. So, I took out my phone and played some music for him, and by this time a good 10 minutes had passed with no parent showing up to look for him. It was cold, for both of us.

In situations like this, my PTSD is triggered. This child was clearly in trouble. I was a child in trouble for years and years and years. I remember walking through the grocery store with Suzy when I was about nine years old and wondering, *Why doesn't some adult come right over and grab me and take me away from this horrible woman? Why doesn't someone save me? How can all these people just walk past?*

Sitting on the playground in the cold, defending this little kid who had no shoes and no coat and no parent, I was suddenly experiencing all the trauma of a lifetime of having no one look after me. Suzy did not take care of me. Bill did not take care of me. My husband, though he paid the bills and did not cheat on me, was not able to be emotionally

171

available to me, and I suffered.

So, I dialed 911 and spoke to the dispatcher who dispatched a sheriff's deputy immediately. I stayed on the phone with the dispatcher. The child walked about 6 feet and stopped. Then he walked back to his original spot. It occurred to me that he had reached a fence, if he were fleeing from someone and coming from a certain direction. Before the officer arrived, a woman came and called for the child. He went to her, but not with any enthusiasm. Between us, the dispatcher and I decided the child was safe enough and the officer did not need to come.

To end the story for you, the officer did not need to come because I knew where the child and woman lived. Even though I did not know the child or know the woman, I was able to follow up and report to the proper people at my church that the incident had occurred. My church was involved with sheltering people who were in need. Clearly, something was not right, and the proper people were made aware.

So, I went to church that morning planning only to worship — normally a neutral experience. Instead, my PTSD was triggered in a big way, and I ended up in tears and having to relive the horror of decades of not having what I needed. I had not lacked shoes; I had not lacked a coat; I had not lacked supervision. But this little boy's deprivation caused me to experience my deprivation, and it hurt a lot.

My behavior is not always the same as the behavior you would expect from someone who does not have a mental illness. Anyone would be upset to see a child who had slipped away from his mother and spent, well, who knows how long outside without shoes and a coat. But I was not just upset; I was traumatized.

There are times when describing myself as mentally ill has had distinctly negative results. There is still a significant stigma associated with being mentally ill. In the eyes of some, saying I am mentally ill makes me dangerous, sometimes dirty, sometimes lacking in intelligence, sometimes childlike, untrustworthy and, this is the hardest one, sometimes suspect just because mental illness is not familiar to the person to whom I am speaking.

I have been open at my church about being mentally ill. Occasionally, I have put a piece of paper in the prayer-requests bowl before the worship service that asks for prayers for me and says, "Jansen asked for prayers. She is learning that her mental illness is much worse than she had thought."

I have also written some articles, now and then, on various topics. One of my favorites was an article called "When Hymns Hurt Me." It was about the theology of hymns that offend me because they express sentiments that are simply not true for me as a mentally ill person. One of my least favorite hymns has a refrain that includes the line, "All I have needed thy hand hath provided." Setting aside the fact that people starve to death, God certainly has not provided me with all that I have needed. I needed a diagnosis three decades earlier than I got it!

With my consent, one of our preachers once read something I had written about being mentally ill. The next Sunday, a precocious child whom I had been teaching to run the sound system during the worship service was suddenly no longer allowed to interact with me. I believe his parents, having learned that I had a mental illness, had decided not to allow him to work with me any longer. It was sad. It hurt.

Only Western medicine has the category "mental illness." But there are parents all over the world at this time – and there have been parents all over the world for as long as there have been human beings – who have inflicted this kind of damage on their children. If persons who have suffered the kind of damage I have suffered have been given any kind of designation, in many cultures in many places and many times, that designation has varied. We have no way to guess whether someone like me would even be singled out as different from the population in some culture in some time and some place.

And if folks like me, by ourselves, or together with some other kind of person or kinds of persons, were lumped together and called "some-thing-or-other" in some place at some time, what might that name be? What would they call people with borderline personality disorder or what would they call people with mental illness in some other place or at some other time or in some other culture?

Was Shakespeare's Juliet right? "What's in a name? That which we call a rose / By any other name would smell as sweet; So Romeo would, were he not Romeo call'd...." What if the "mentally ill" were called "exceptional"? What if they were called "bizarre"?

The designation might be neutral. It might carry negative connotations. It might carry positive connotations. It might carry some mixture of meanings.

I would like to believe that this kind of damage is less likely to happen when society is organized less around the nuclear family. Also, the more that extended families and villages or church groups or other close-knit social groups are involved in parenting children, so that it is not just the mother and the father who have their eye on each child, the more this kind of damage cannot happen. If there had been a grandma or neighbor or a pastor who had regularly held me and cuddled me as a baby, my chances would have been much better. But I was isolated in the house with Suzy.

The crucial time is from birth to one-year-old — not that the damage cannot be ameliorated significantly with excellent parenting beginning at one-year-old — it absolutely can. I lived in a state of deprivation until I was, um, well…for a long time.

Let's support new parents! Let's encourage new parents to feel free to ask for help. Let's be sure all new parents know that parenting is a very, very difficult job.

And for those people who may have been damaged, I want to say that many paths lead to reduced suffering. Western medicine is one of them. But there are many others.

Keep thinking about your situation. Try something new.

I believe things can get better.

Persist.

How Should We Treat Persons Who Are Apparently Different?

[Reprinted, with permission, from Gross and Cooper, 2020, Apparently Different.]

MY CHURCH FAMILY, my sisters- and brothers-in-Christ at the UCC church where I've worshiped for 30 years, experience me as different from others. I have a very serious mental illness: borderline personality disorder.

Although borderline personality disorder has different manifestations (of course), it is almost always a "listen to me" illness. I have noticed that I don't have the ability to chat. In every social situation, I talk about something that is important to me. It seems I can only talk about my passionate interests.

How am I apparently different? My conversation is always intense. I don't have a light, chatty mode. At the church coffee time, people talking to me hear about my mental illness and my marriage and my thoughts on the sermon we just heard. When I am paying for my sandwich at a deli, the cashier hears my thoughts on her tattoo and the importance of expressing ourselves with our clothing, hairstyles, make-up, and body adornment.

To give credit where it's due, many people respond positively to having an interaction that has some real depth where they expected an interaction that was simply polite and surface-y. But sometimes people perceive that they are speaking to someone who has a mental illness; sometimes people perceive that my intensity is an indication that I am not well.

They are correct. I am not well.

It is not unreasonable for someone to be wary of me when they perceive that I am not well. Let me say how I would like to be treated by a person whom I encounter casually who figures out that they are talking to somebody who is not mentally well:

1. I would wish that people could assess whether I am dangerous or not.
2. I wish people would carefully choose the type of reply they give to me.
3. I wish people had a context for understanding my behavior.

Am I dangerous?

When we encounter someone in public who does not interact with us within our socially acceptable boundaries, when we encounter someone who is inappropriately intense, we are wise to be careful. An inability (or unwillingness) to follow society's rules is, in fact, a serious concern. Is this person, we might wonder, someone whose inappropriate behavior is only verbal? Or might they also misbehave in ways that are dangerous?

As it happens, my unexpectedly intense conversation is not a reflection of any inability to follow society's other rules. I do not go into a coffee shop and sit down at a table where somebody is busily working on his laptop and strike up a conversation that is unwelcome. That would be a behavior that is both physical and verbal — I would be violating society's rule that a person in a coffee shop working on their computer should not be disturbed. In my subculture of American culture, currently, sitting in a coffee shop working on your computer communicates that you are busy and are not available to socialize.

My violations of society's rules don't extend to physical behaviors. I don't follow people to their cars. I don't pinch the cheeks of their children. I am not dangerous unless someone is endangered by words.

I am happy to say that the content of my intense conversations rarely harms people with words that attack or criticize. But let's keep in mind that my comments to some young cashier about her tattoo may harm her even if I only say that I like it. We do not always know if our words are helpful, neutral, or harmful.

Do people choose their replies?

In a social situation, most people operate on autopilot. Most people have a set of, maybe, 100 sentences or phrases they use when they are chatting. At church coffee time, many people pull up and fling out some sentence or phrase that seems to fit the situation. Most people do not choose with any care the reply they give to me when we talk.

I had a conversation with a neighbor who is a physician. We were discussing a child in our neighborhood who had needed some emergency medical care. I said that I had intervened, without the family's knowledge, to get social services for early childhood intervention into the home to address the needs of the older child. His response was, "Well, there's nothing we can do about it."

This man was simply handing me a sentence that he speaks in social situations in which he does not know quite what to say. Faced with the intensity of my conversation, in a situation where many people would be chatting in a light manner, he produced a wildly inappropriate response. It was inappropriate because he had, in fact, been instrumental in getting the emergency medical care that may have saved the life of the infant sister. Obviously, it is not the case that "there's nothing we can do about it."

My suffering, as a person who is different, would be reduced if our society had an expectation that people choose their words carefully. Our culture's willingness to tolerate inane, light social responses is a problem for me as a mentally ill person.

Do people have a context for understanding my behavior?

One of my favorite sentences is: "Depression is the common cold of mental illness." Most people who are familiar with mental illness call up, in their minds, an image of a depressed person when they think of a mentally ill person. Also, many people have heard of schizophrenia and bipolar disorder. Depression, schizophrenia, and bipolar disorder are all treatable. Most people with depression can take medication and go to therapy and be substantially free of symptoms after a year or a couple of years. Indeed, depressions that are not mental illness are a normal part of any normal life. Everyone will feel depressed after the death of a beloved parent. So, when people hear the phrase *mental illness*, they often think of something that is treated and then goes away. If they have any understanding of persistent mental illness, they may well think of schizophrenia which, for many people, can be substantially mitigated with medication.

180

Borderline personality disorder has no cure. Some medications help some patients. Unlike the treatment of schizophrenia, the treatment of borderline personality disorder does not include some vital medication. The medications doctors prescribe most often for schizophrenia are antipsychotics. For many patients, they ease symptoms such as delusions and hallucinations. There is no medication for BPD that similarly eases the symptoms.[1] Certain behaviors associated with borderline personality disorder — behaviors that are very disruptive in the life of the sufferer and the lives of their families — can be "treated." Dialectical behavioral therapy (DBT) is an approach that has been successful at helping people with borderline personality disorder lead a life worth living. If, for example, someone with borderline personality disorder is getting some relief from their suffering by gambling, but their gambling keeps them in a state of perpetual poverty, DBT can help them stop the behavior that is making their life worse.

This is no small thing! But DBT does not cure borderline personality disorder. One does not stop having borderline personality disorder and one does not stop suffering the internal pain that is a daily part of borderline personality disorder. The success of DBT has been in its ability to help sufferers create a life worth living.

My suffering would be reduced if people whom I encounter were aware that some mental illness is lifelong and is uncurable. I have been in therapy for 40 years. All the tips and tricks available to a person with borderline personality disorder for managing the illness have been presented to me. I have tried everything. I manage my illness very well, actually. Sometimes this fools people into thinking that I am more mentally healthy than I am.

---

1   "Overall, meta-analysis provides little evidence to support the use of antidepressant medication in BPD outside episodes of major depression. However, there is evidence for the use of both mood stabilizers and antipsychotic medications for the treatment of specific aspects of the disorder." Olabi, Bayanne and Hall, Jeremy (2010) Borderline personality disorder: current drug treatments and future prospects, *Therapeutic Advances in Chronic Disease* 1(2): 59-66

A woman at my church, in response to a conversation in which I told her how seriously ill I am (mentally ill), sent me an email in which she said, "You stated that your psychiatrist left the HMO because she couldn't go along with their rules, that she charges $650/hour in private practice and you're seeing her 4x/week. That set off red flags for me. First, I've never heard of any doctor charging that much. I imagine you heard _her_ story. I would urge you to investigate her leaving the HMO further and perhaps make further inquiries."

This woman's response to my (good) news that, since I no longer have managed care at this HMO, I now am able to see a therapist who is a psychiatrist and that she, the psychiatrist, has recognized how sick I am and how much help I need, was to send me an email in which she questioned my choice of a doctor. This woman from my church simply does not have a context in which to understand the seriousness of my mental illness. I would guess that she doesn't know anyone else who has needed therapy for 40 years. I would guess that she doesn't know anyone else who needs to see a therapist four times a week. Unless this woman, my sister-in-Christ, is unkind, I would guess that she simply has no context in which to understand the information that I gave her.

How different it would be to receive an email that said, "I was so sorry to hear that your suffering is so intense. I was so sorry to hear that your mental illness is so serious that you see your psychiatrist four times per week." I wish there were a greater awareness in our society that profoundly mentally ill people **are** part of the population and may even be attending church with us.

How, then, shall we treat people whom we encounter who are different — whose differences are apparent from their behavior? The more we understand the wide variety of kinds of human beings there are in the world, the better we will be able to treat people well. In the grocery store, we see mostly people who are well-groomed, who do not smell bad. But sometimes we see someone who does not have a home where they can wash their clothes and shower. And sometimes we see someone who **does** have a home but is not able to wash their clothes and shower. And, maybe more often than we know, we see someone whose clothes are clean who has daily seizures, or who is struggling because they hear voices. The more we understand that the people we see may be facing invisible challenges, the better we will be able to treat people well, especially when their challenges become apparent.

APPENDIX

A Few Select Resources

The National Suicide Prevention Lifeline
https://suicidepreventionlifeline.org
800-273-8255
This is a resource for people in distress as well as for the prevention of suicide. You do not need to feel suicidal to call this line. You can call with concerns of all kinds. In addition to their phone line, at the URL you can access their text chat.

NAMI
https://nami.org/
The National Alliance on Mental Illness
NAMI is the National Alliance on Mental Illness, the nation's largest grassroots mental health organization dedicated to building better lives for the millions of Americans affected by mental illness.

MentalHealth.gov
https://www.mentalhealth.gov/
MentalHealth.gov provides one-stop access to U.S. government mental health and mental health problems information.

Borderline Personality Disorder Pages at the National Institute of Mental Health

https://www.nimh.nih.gov/health/topics/borderline-personality-disorder/index.shtml

The National Institute of Mental Health (NIMH) is the lead federal agency for research on mental disorders.

Google Scholar

https://scholar.google.com/

Google Scholar provides a simple way to broadly search for scholarly literature. From one place, you can search across many disciplines and sources: articles, theses, books, abstracts, and court opinions, from academic publishers, professional societies, online repositories, universities, and other web sites.

Marsha Linehan's Behavioral Tech

https://behavioraltech.org/

Marsha Linehan invented DBT, Dialectical Behavioral Therapy. Behavioral Tech trains mental health care providers and treatment teams who work with complex and severely disordered populations to use compassionate, scientifically valid treatments and to implement and evaluate these treatments in their practice setting.

About the Author

JANSEN VEE IS a woman with a very mathematical and analytical mind who lives in the Pacific Northwest. She is retired from a 20-year teaching career. She especially enjoyed the terms during which she got to teach college students about Turing machines, conceptual machines that model computation.

Now Jansen is spending her time growing as a human person, making her homeowners' association a kinder and gentler organization, writing about issues close to her heart and doing the many boring things required to keep her skin and lungs happy. Jansen is a life-long liberal Christian and is 60 years old.

You can read more about Jansen Vee at www.jansenvee.com. Email to Jansen can be sent from the website also.

Review *Watching Myself*

READERS AND AUTHORS depend heavily on the information received from reviewers of books, especially at the largest supplier of books in America, Amazon.com. It would be appreciated if you would review this book there, or at other such sites, whether briefly or in some depth.

Comments concerning *Watching Myself Be Borderline* are welcome at Jansen Vee's author website, www.jansenvee.com. The website has additional resources, some blog articles and more information about the author.

9 781977 231871